Teammate Tuesdays

Volume VI

Another Year of Good Teammate Musings

LANCE LOYA

CAGER HAUS
PUBLISHING

ISBN-13: 979-8-9881879-0-5

www.coachloya.com

Design and publishing by Cager Haus.
Cover image by Kutsal Lenger, Dreamstime.com.

For Laken and Lakota…may you always be good teammates.

Contents

Acknowledgements

Another year leads to another book! I want to once again offer a special thank you to Wendy Clouner for suggesting that I start a blog. Although I wasn't initially receptive to your suggestion, I am glad I eventually acquiesced. Here we are six volumes later and still going strong. I also want to express my gratitude to Rachel Loya and Cindy Davis for your continued support and recommendations.

I would also like the thank my Good Teammate Factory clients and the online community members who read blogs, listen to podcasts, like and share social media posts, and offer invaluable feedback and encouragement. You are the fuel that powers the *Be a Good Teammate* movement.

Introduction

Welcome to *Teammate Tuesdays Volume VI*! Being able to assemble another book of this nature makes my heart smile. Let me share with you how the *Teammate Tuesdays* book series came to be.

Once upon a time, I set out on a journey to discover an answer to the question: *What does it mean to be a good teammate?* Everybody belongs to some type of team. Maybe it's an actual sports team, or maybe it's the place where you work, the community you live in, the church you attend, or simply your family. Ultimately, the success of any team depends on the capacity of its members to be good teammates. But what specifically does being a "good" teammate entail?

My journey began with the publication of a children's book called *Be a Good Teammate*. The book revolved around the idea that good teammates do three things: care, share, and listen. I wrote that book with the sole intention of conveying

1

some fatherly advice to my daughters, who, at the time, were learning to read.

The publication of *Be a Good Teammate* unexpectedly set into motion a sequence of events that changed the trajectory of my life and led me to the realization that the world needs more good teammates—kind, mindful, unselfish individuals who put the needs of their teams ahead of any self-centered agendas. This belief transcends sports and applies to all varieties of teams.

Eventually, exploring the art of being a good teammate became my life's work. Somewhere along the way, I decided to heed the advice of a trusted friend and share my discoveries—my *musings*—in a weekly blog. I called the blog "Teammate Tuesdays" and posted a new entry every Tuesday morning.

As the blog's following grew, subscribers began reaching out to me about the possibility of making the content available in print form. They wanted to give the blog as a gift to their friends, families, and teams. To accommodate the recurring requests, I turned the entire first year of my blog into a book titled *Teammate Tuesdays: A Year of Good Teammate Musings*.

The book you're presently reading is a compilation of the entire sixth year of my blog. Like the previous volumes, this book will provide you with an abundance of "good teammate" stories, observations, and insights—each intended to make you think about what kind of teammate you are and how you can inspire others to become better teammates.

It should be noted that this book is written in a more informal, conversational tone—the way blogs typically are. Each post (chapter) was written as an independent entity. With a few minor exceptions, like the removal of embedded hyperlinks and the addition of appropriate citations, the content has not been altered from how it originally appeared online.

Topics covered in this year's volume include virality, gallantry, and redemption. There are stories about Taylor Swift, grizzly bears, and the origins of National Be a Good Teammate Day. Readers will also be introduced to a variety of different types of teammates, like Ketchup Teammates, Sandpaper Teammates, and Pink Shirt Teammates.

I continue to like the idea of assembling an entire year's worth of posts in a book format. The content is worth sharing in an alternative medium. Not everyone who can benefit from the message reads blogs. Some people still prefer to hold a physical book in their hands. Putting the blog in book form makes it possible to share the message with a broader audience.

A book is also a convenient way to bring up to speed those who may be joining the Good Teammate movement *already in progress*. The format allows you to experience your own journey of discovery, at your own pace. You don't have to wait until next week to find out what topic I am going to cover in my blog. You can read the chapters as fast or slow as you desire. It's like binge reading a blog.

I am often asked two questions: *Why Tuesdays?* and *Why doesn't the first chapter start on January 1?*

We all have seasons to our lives. For some, it's spring, summer, fall, and winter. For those involved in sports, it's preseason, regular season, postseason, and offseason. I wrote my initial blog post at the end of April, coinciding with what was at that time considered to be the start of my offseason— the ideal time to start new endeavors. I have consistently added a new post every week since then, which is why the first chapter doesn't start on January 1.

Why Tuesdays? I am a fan of Mitch Albom's memoir *Tuesday's with Morrie.* In the book, he chronicles the wisdom acquired from his weekly visits with his former sociology professor Morrie Swartz, who is dying from ALS. The name *Teammate Tuesdays* was a tip of the hat of sorts to Albom's book and its touching premise. But that's not the only reason. I also believe that Tuesdays are generally the best days for personal and professional development.

Wednesdays mark the middle of the week. It's *hump day.* You've come to the realization that you better put your nose to the grindstone and get busy or you're going to run out of time.

Thursdays still have some of the same urgency to get your work done as Wednesdays. But by Thursday afternoon, you are starting to set your sights on the weekend.

Fridays are the day to wrap up loose ends and then coast through the rest of the day. It's the end of the traditional work week, so you're reluctant to start any new projects. You may also feel burned out by Friday and not necessarily motivated to engage in anything mentally taxing.

Saturdays are spent catching up on chores, like cutting grass and doing laundry. Saturdays are additionally a day for recreation and seeking fun.

Sundays are family time. You're ready to relax and spend quality time with your friends and family. If you're struggling with your job, you'll probably spend Sunday evening stressing about having to go back to work the next day. Professional development isn't a high priority on Sundays.

Mondays are consumed with playing catch up. You're trying to finish all the work you didn't complete—but should have—last week. You are probably also being bombarded with everything that was delivered over the weekend. You have an endless amount of pressing emails and phone calls to return. By the time Mondays are over, you are exhausted.

Which brings us to Tuesdays. You are tired from playing catch up on Monday and not anxious to put in another intense day of work. You convince yourself that you still have the rest of the week to get your work done. Why start today? Tuesdays are the perfect day for self-reflection and an investment in self-improvement.

Sound familiar? If so, then you've come to the right place. Every day is *Tuesday* in this book.

I hope you enjoy my collection of good teammate musings. My wish is for them to inspire you to become a better version of yourself and to equip you with the tools to help others do the same.

Good Teammate Move

/ ˈgu̇d – ˈtēm · māt – müv / **noun.** a kind, generous, selfless act committed by an individual member of a team for the sole purpose of helping his or her team.

The term *good teammate move* appears numerous times throughout this book. The concept was first introduced in the inaugural volume of *Teammate Tuesdays*. While the context surrounding the term generally provides sufficient understanding of its meaning, consider the following: Dancers have moves. They plié, pirouette, and lean-and-dab. The more dance moves they have, the better dancer they are. Basketball players have moves. They spin, crossover, and go behind their backs. The more moves they have, the better player they are. The same rationale applies to good teammates. The more good teammate moves you make, the better teammate you are.

Wabi-Sabi Enlightenment
APRIL 26

I concede that I may be a little biased, but I think my dining room table is among the most beautiful pieces of furniture I have ever seen. I love its rich colors, varying textures, and—most of all—its unique backstory.

While you may be able to find tables at Pottery Barn or Crate & Barrel that are similar in appearance, none of them possess an accompanying backstory like mine.

In the book *Building Good Teammates*, I write about my unusual childhood. My family ran a hotel in the Allegheny Mountains that was built to resemble an ocean liner. In its heyday, the S.S. Grandview Ship Hotel welcomed the who's who of the world's rich and famous.

Charlie Chaplin, Thomas Edison, Henry Ford, Greta Garbo, President Calvin Coolidge, and many others partied on the hotel's famous wooden decks during their stays.

Sadly, the hotel fell into disrepair and burned down in 2001. But before its demise, I managed to salvage several boards from the ship's main deck and used them to build my dining room table.

We recently had people over to our house for dinner. One of our guests, Ben, who is of Japanese descent, was particularly fascinated by our table.

A sign hanging in our dining room lists the names of famous people, including those mentioned above, who have "walked on our table." The sign is intended to be a tongue-in-cheek way of prompting further conversation about the table's origins. Ben didn't seem impressed by nor interested in the sign. He just kept smiling, stroking his hand across the top of the table, while softly repeating, "Wabi-sabi."

I didn't understand what he was saying. To me, it sounded like "wasabi" or "white sake." I felt inclined to tell Ben that we weren't going to be serving either of those at dinner. He laughed and then repeated himself again in a slow, over-enunciated, elongated manner: "No, waaaaaaaaaabbbbiiii-sssaaaaaaaaabbbbiii."

He explained that *wabi-sabi* is a Japanese concept that translates into beauty being found through imperfection.

The deck boards, now more than 100 years old, used to construct the table are riddled with hundreds of nail holes, nicks, cracks, and stains, all of which contribute to the table's rustic beauty. Without those imperfections, the table wouldn't be nearly as striking.

The concept of wabi-sabi applies to the art of being a good teammate. Apart from their unwavering desire to serve the best interests of their team, good teammates are not perfect.

They have flaws, shortcomings, and weaknesses. And they sometimes make mistakes.

Their beauty, however, is found in their ability to own their flaws, overcome their shortcomings, work on their weaknesses, and evolve from their mistakes.

Good teammates embrace their imperfections and the imperfections of their fellow teammates. Bear in mind that embracing an imperfection isn't the same as tolerating behaviors that are counter to the team's culture.

Artist Leonard Koren described wabi-sabi as appreciating "the beauty of things imperfect, impermanent, and incomplete." Koren's description captures both the resilience and continuous evolution of good teammates—individuals who understand that which does not kill can not only make you stronger but can also make you beautiful.

As always…Good teammates care. Good teammates share. Good teammates listen. Go be a good teammate.

A photo of the dining room table referenced in this chapter is viewable at www.coachloya.com/wabi-sabi-enlightenment/

Candy's Crusade
MAY 3

On May 3, 1980, a thirteen-year-old youth softball player named Cari Lightner was killed by a drunk driver in Fair Oaks, California. Cari and a friend were walking to a church carnival when Clarence Bush's car swerved out of control and struck the teen from behind.

In the days that followed, Candy Lightner, Cari's mother, would come to learn that Bush had a lengthy history of arrests for driving impaired, including a similar hit-and-run drunk driving charge from less than a week earlier.

An investigating officer told Candy that drunk driving was rarely prosecuted with severity and that Bush would likely receive little to no jail time for his offense—an atrocity that outraged the grieving mother.

Determined to spare other parents from having to experience the pain of losing a child to such an avoidable horror and to right what she believed to be an unacceptable wrong, Candy Lightner founded Mothers Against Drunk

Driving (MADD). Her crusade to end drunk driving offers three invaluable "good teammate" lessons:

1. Don't underestimate the impact of one good teammate. MADD has grown to become one of the largest and most influential non-profits in the entire world. At the time of her daughter's death, Candy Lightner was a divorced, single mother of three, supporting her family as a part-time real estate agent. She wasn't wealthy. She wasn't famous. She had no influential platform. But she was motivated to create change.

That motivation led Candy and her MADD volunteers to successfully lobby for mandatory minimum sentences for repeat drunk driving offenders, raise the legal drinking age to 21, and lower the legal blood alcohol content level to .08 nationally.

Too often team members default to apathy because they mistakenly think their individual efforts won't make a difference. Candy Lightner is proof of the impact one motivated individual can make.

2. With the right mindset, tragedy can give birth to victory. Candy turned her anger into action. Instead of a *woe-is-me* attitude, she embraced a *we-can-do-better* mindset. She used the tragedy of her daughter's death to save the lives of countless others.

In 1980, the year her daughter was killed, over 27,000 drunk driving fatalities occurred in the United States. That number has steadily declined since MADD's inception, with the most recent statistics showing drunk driving fatalities dropping an astounding 65 percent since then.

Competitive teams will inevitably experience losses, setbacks, and disappointments. Whenever these happen, good teammates don't wallow in self-pity, point fingers, or abandon ship. They use the experience to bring their teams closer together. Their approach turns setbacks into comebacks.

3. Relentlessness leads to cultural changes. Of all the good that has come from Candy's crusade, the shift in cultural perspective toward drunk driving is the most profound. Past generations viewed drunk driving through a much softer lens.

Today, designated drivers, self-restraint, and harsh penalties for DUI offenders are the expectation. Alerting others to sobriety checkpoint locations is now considered taboo and will get you chastised on social media.

A relentless commitment to embracing team standards will lead to a positive change in team culture. Good teammates are catalysts for change because they dedicate themselves to consistently doing what's best for their team.

As always…Good teammates care. Good teammates share. Good teammates listen. Go be a good teammate.

The statistics on drunk driving fatalities referenced above can be found at https://www.nhtsa.gov/risky-driving/drunk-driving

The Crumpled Aspect
MAY 10

Several years ago, a story circulated on the internet about a teacher and a clever bullying exercise involving a crumpled piece of paper. Although the story's exact origins were somewhat of a mystery, its lesson resonated with readers.

The crumpled paper exercise recently resurfaced on TikTok and is now trending with an entirely new audience. If you're unfamiliar with the original story, it goes like this:

A teacher instructs her students to remove a piece of paper from their notebooks. She tells them to crumple the paper up, stomp on it, and rub it into the dirty floor. They can mess the paper up anyway they want, so long as they don't tear it.

She then tells her students to unfold the paper, smooth it out, and examine how scarred and dirty it now is. Her final instructions require the students to apologize to the crumpled paper for what they did to it.

The point of her exercise was to get her students to realize the lasting damage bullying causes. Even though they had

15

apologized and tried to fix the paper, the "scars" remained. The teacher tells her students that the same happens whenever they bully another student.

Though touching and offering an important bullying insight, the crumpled paper exercise is incomplete because it neglects to include a lesson for the paper—an aspect that has relevance to the art of being a good teammate.

Despite being damaged and scarred, the crumpled piece of paper should be reminded that it still has plenty of value.

The paper can still be written on, made into a paper airplane, folded into an origami swan, or cut into a beautiful paper snowflake. In fact, because of its stains and crumpled texture, the scarred piece of paper has the potential to become uniquely beautiful in a way that an *unscarred* piece of paper never can.

Jealous teammates and narcissistic leaders will sometimes resort to bullying to advance their agendas. They'll leverage their position, popularity, or power to wreak havoc on their victim's life, which indirectly wreaks havoc on their team's culture.

While increasing awareness and improving empathy is certainly beneficial to curbing bullying, equipping the bullying recipient with confidence and effective counter-bullying strategies is equally beneficial, especially since the victim's response to being bullied can wreak even greater havoc on a team.

Bullied teammates can become bitter, jaded, cynical, and withdrawn—all of which lead to apathy and contribute to a toxic team environment.

Good teammates don't bully other members of their team, nor do they allow themselves and their fellow teammates to be devalued by bullying. They resist the clutches of apathy by refusing to be held back by their scars.

As always…Good teammates care. Good teammates share. Good teammates listen. Go be a good teammate.

The TikTok video referenced above can be viewed at https://vm.tiktok.com/ZTdpeK1SU/

The Pina Colada Problem
MAY 17

While speaking to a group of human resource professionals, someone in the audience asked me if I had a recommendation for handling a problem that she was having with two of her team members.

She explained that she had two managers on her team who used to work well together. But lately, these two managers were constantly "locking horns." Neither was willing to compromise or see issues from the other's perspective.

What frustrated her the most about the situation, however, was that each of the managers shared the same passion for their team's success. They were both talented, dedicated, humble, and hard working—and valued those qualities in others. She wondered if these two managers realized how much they had in common.

I told her it sounded like she had a *pina colada problem.* Assuming that I meant her situation called for an adult beverage, the rest of the audience laughed at my response.

When the laughter died, I assured everyone that I wasn't referring to the beverage, I was referring to the song.

Rupert Holmes topped the pop charts in the late seventies with a song titled "Escape." The song was about a man whose current relationship grows stale. One night while reading the newspaper, the man happens upon a personal ad from a woman looking for a companion, who among other things, likes pina coladas. Because of the song's catchy chorus, it's often known as "The Pina Colada Song."

If you like piña coladas
And gettin' caught in the rain
If you're not into yoga
If you have half a brain
If you like makin' love at midnight
In the dunes on the cape
Then I'm the love that you've looked for
Write to me and escape

Intrigued, the man replies to the ad and arranges to meet the woman "at a bar called O'Malley's" to "plan (their) escape."

The song's final verse reveals the man's surprise when he arrives at O'Malley's and discovers the woman from the ad to be his current lover. The two of them realize in that moment that they already have in each other what they seek in a relationship. Much like the couple in the pina colada song, relationships between teammates can sometimes grow stale. The familiarity of working alongside the same individual for extended periods can lead to indifference. Whenever this happens, the proverbial grass starts to look greener elsewhere and planning an "escape" seems increasingly more appealing.

I told the audience member that she needed to remind her managers of how much they had in common—especially their mutual passion for their team's success. I recommended that she start by independently asking each of them three simple questions:

1. Is your team's success important to you?
2. Are you committed to your team?
3. Are you willing to sacrifice for your team?

If her description of the two managers is accurate, I suspect both will answer the questions the same way. Once she gets them to remember that they are both working toward the same objective, she will be able to delve deeper into what specifically is causing their indifference.

Alcoholic drinks like pina coladas have a reputation for being social lubricants. A reminder of shared values can function the same way for driven, committed teammates. In an interview with *Songfacts*, Rupert Holmes said his pina colada song was originally set to be titled "People Need Other People." Though not nearly as catchy, the original title does capture a "good teammate" insight: No team members achieve success without the help of their team.

As always…Good teammates care. Good teammates share. Good teammates listen. Go be a good teammate.

*The full Songfacts interview referenced above can be found at https://www.songfacts.com/blog/interviews/rupert-holmes-pina-colada-song

Commencing With Purpose
MAY 24

Commencement season is upon us. It's time to don caps and gowns, cue "Pomp and Circumstance," and dispense wisdom through the time-honored tradition of commencement addresses. *New York Times* best-selling author Bruce Feiler analyzed one hundred commencement addresses. In his bi-weekly newsletter about navigating life's ups and downs, "The Nonlinear Life," Feiler identified four tips to be present in all of them:

1. Dream Big
2. Work Hard
3. Make Mistakes
4. Be Kind

Since reading Feiler's findings, I've been thinking about how each of those tips applies to being a good teammate—and I'm convinced they all do.

Good teammates dream big. They aspire for their teams to achieve on the highest levels. Scaling the heights of success requires ambition and a readiness to ignore all the reasons that could prevent success from becoming a reality.

Good teammates work hard. They don't know the meaning of the word lazy. Showing grit and grinding out a team goal is an intrinsic part of their very existence.

Good teammates are willing to make mistakes. They understand that mistakes are part of the growth process. Applying the knowledge gained from a mistake leads to progress, prevents repeating the same mistake (something good teammates avoid), and sparks innovation.

Good teammates are kind. They consider the impact their words and actions have on others. Extending friendliness, generosity, and concern facilitates the type of caring team culture that fosters success.

What binds good teammates to these four practices? Service and purpose. Good teammates dream big, work hard, are willing to make mistakes, and behave kindly—*for their team*.

That important addendum provides context to the tips and keeps them from becoming dysfunctional habits.

Without purpose, dreaming big can turn into disillusionment. Without purpose, working hard can turn into burnout. Without purpose, making mistakes can turn into apathy. And without purpose, being kind can turn into being taken advantage of.

Service leads to purpose. Purpose leads to happiness. What better advice could any person pass on to a graduate than a proven strategy for acquiring happiness?

As always…Good teammates care. Good teammates share. Good teammates listen. Go be a good teammate.

*Bruce Feiler's The Nonlinear Life newsletter referenced above can be found at https://brucefeiler.bulletin.com/i-analyzed-100-commencement-speeches-these-are-the-4-tips-they-all-share

Ollie's Five/Five Rules
MAY 31

Holiday gatherings are great for meeting interesting people. I had the pleasure of meeting a fascinating octogenarian named Ollie over the Memorial Day weekend. And I am glad I did.

Ollie was full of vigor and possessed a zeal for life like few humans I have ever encountered. He embodied Dos Equis' *The Most Interesting Man in the World*, and his stories captivated my attention.

While we were chatting, I happened to notice that Ollie's wristwatch had stopped working. I pointed to his watch and mentioned that its battery must've died.

"Oh, this watch hasn't worked in ages. I don't worry much about time anymore," Ollie said.

I found his reply to be curious and wondered why he bothered to wear a watch. Was he a Jimmy Buffett fan, believing it was always five o'clock somewhere? When I asked, Ollie told me that he deliberately leaves his watch stuck on five o'clock to remind himself of his "five/five rules"— the "secret" to his vitality.

Fifty-five rules? To me, that seemed like a lot of rules to live by.

I suspect Ollie sensed my skepticism. He clarified, "No, not fifty-five rules. F-I-V-E/F-I-V-E rules." He explained that his life was guided by five rules, each involving the number five:

Rule #1: If it won't matter in five years, don't waste more the five minutes worrying about it. I have heard this rule before and it resonates with me. Sometimes referred to as the "5×5 Rule" or the "Five Minute Rule," the concept keeps pettiness from causing people to lose perspective.

Rule #2: If five years from now you're going to regret not doing it, start doing it now. Life is largely about living with regrets. The end of your life will be more enjoyable if you can lighten your regret load along the way. Ollie pointed out that you can make up for lost money and lost sleep, but it's hard to make up for lost opportunities.

Rule #3: You don't need more than five of anything. Moderation matters. As the saying goes, too much of anything can be a bad thing. Excess stymies creativity, creates clutter, and plateaus the soul. Conversely, moderation enables efficiency, sparks ingenuity, and invigorates the soul.

Rule #4: Refuse to allow yourself to be content with being the same version of yourself that you were five years ago. Seek opportunities for growth—mentally, physically, and emotionally. A commitment to lifelong learning keeps the mind sharp and the soul green. You start dying the moment you stop growing.

Rule #5: Give yourself a high-five every day. This rule is akin to "celebrating your victories." Studies have shown that gratitude positively impacts your health. Studies have also shown that people respond positively to recognition. Make a point to acknowledge the daily challenges you overcame and thank yourself for persevering.

Nobody offers a more sincere perspective on life than someone nearing its end. Ollie's rules not only provide a path for a happy life, they provide a blueprint for building a mindset that can help you be a better teammate.

As always…Good teammates care. Good teammates share. Good teammates listen. Go be a good teammate.

The Power of Virality
JUNE 7

In my book *The WE Gear*, I describe the five key behaviors of good teammates—Active, Loyal, Invested, Viral, and Empathetic. Those behaviors are crucial to maximizing teamwork, especially the fourth. I had an interesting opportunity last week to witness firsthand how true this is.

A group of Texas Head Start and Early Head Start professionals used *The WE Gear* for a leadership book study this year and brought me in to speak at their organization's annual year-end retreat.

Head Start is an amazing program that provides services to underprivileged children and families. They do important work and their organization is filled with kind, caring people.

Early morning engagements can be tricky. Getting people—even kind, caring ones–to be enthusiastic at that hour can be like drawing blood from a stone.

The program's leader enthusiastically welcomed everyone to the retreat, but it took her several rounds of "Good

Morning…I said GOOOOD MOOORNING" just to generate a minor uptick in the room's energy level.

Before introducing me to speak, the book study team presented the findings from a poll they conducted during their study. As they relayed the data, which I found to be both fascinating and insightful, they solicited feedback from the audience.

But the audience still seemed lethargic and reluctant to engage—until, a bubbly woman named Pauline stood up to speak.

Pauline smiled, laughed, and spoke with passion. More importantly, though, her response triggered everyone else to smile, laugh, and passionately nod their heads in agreement. Pauline's fervor was contagious, and it changed the temperature of the entire room.

A few moments later, a woman named Tamika stood and provided a similarly enthusiastic testimonial. Her words moved the audience to joyful tears. If Pauline's fervor got the ball rolling, Tamika's was the equivalent of, "Ball, I'm not going to let you stop rolling. In fact, I'm going to make you roll faster."

By the time I was introduced to speak, the room was filled with kind, caring…lively, enthusiastic individuals—eager to hear about the art of being a good teammate. Pauline and Tamika warmed up the audience and made my job exponentially easier. (*Good teammate move* on their part!)

Virality—the state of being viral—leads to momentum. Sometimes all a team needs to get moving in the right direction is a little virality from one or two of its team members.

Unfortunately, people don't always appreciate the power of virality to the extent that they should. They write off a teammate's virality as "that's just who that teammates is." But there's more to virality than natural personality.

Being viral requires courage, a willingness to be judged, and a willingness to step outside of your comfort zone—*for the benefit of your team.*

Everyone has the capacity to be viral. Those who wish to make a difference on their teams choose to be viral. If you've got teammates like Pauline and Tamika on your team, don't take them for granted. Embrace their virality and allow it to inspire you.

As always…Good teammates care. Good teammates share. Good teammates listen. Go be a good teammate.

A One Percent Teammate
JUNE 14

Several decades ago, I attended a coaching clinic in Nashville, Tennessee hosted by legendary coach Don Meyer at what was then David Lipscomb University. I was still a college student-athlete at the time but went to the clinic in anticipation of one day embarking on a coaching career.

Coach Meyer was a pioneer in terms of providing professional development opportunities for coaches. He shared his knowledge generously, passionately, and creatively. If you'll pardon the cliché, he *put on a clinic* on how to put on a clinic.

The car ride from my home to Nashville was fourteen hours each way. It wasn't an easy trip to make. I didn't have a lot money at the time, nor an especially reliable car. But I am glad I made that trip because it had a profound impact on my life.

While Coach Meyer's clinic included the usual discussions about strategies, Xs and Os, and effective game management, he said something in between those discussions that resonated with me more than anything else: "Always be a quarter friend."

Coach Meyer asked attendees to think about how they lived their lives and what kind of a friend they were to others. If someone was in trouble, would that individual use their last quarter to call you for help?

That question has never strayed far from my mind.

The evolution of technology dates the context of Coach Meyer's words. We barely use coins anymore and payphones are practically extinct. Having to make a phone call by dropping a "quarter" into a metal box is beyond the comprehension of younger generations.

Although the context of being a *quarter friend* has become obsolete, the concept certainly has not. The deeper I explore the art of being a good teammate, the more truthful I find this statement to be.

Good teammates want to be *quarter friends* to their fellow teammates. They want to be the one you call in a crisis. They want to be the one you know will not let you down. They want to be the one you know will be relentless in helping you solve your problem.

And most of all, they will not object to you calling and entrusting them with this responsibility.

I'm not certain that a modern-day equivalent exists for the term *quarter friend*. I suppose the closest we can come is a *one percent friend*, or more applicably, a *one percent teammate* (i.e., if someone needed help and their cell phone battery was down to its last one percent, would that individual call you?).

I've discovered that the happiest people I know take genuine pride in being the type of teammate who embodies this concept. They choose to wear the responsibility like a badge of honor.

The problem with failing teams is often that they don't have enough *one percent teammates*. Too many of their members resent being inconvenienced, aren't invested in others, and make their reluctance to help anybody but themselves readily known.

Those teams' fortunes would change, however, if they increased their percentage of *one percent teammates*.

As always…Good teammates care. Good teammates share. Good teammates listen. Go be a good teammate.

Lyrical Lessons
JUNE 21

Last week, Sir Paul McCartney celebrated his eightieth birthday. You don't have to be a diehard McCartney fan to appreciate his music or have a deep-level of respect for all he has accomplished.

In honor of the Beatles bassist's birthday, here are eight iconic Paul McCartney songs and their accompanying lyrics (one for each decade of his life) with lessons that pertain to the art of being a good teammate:

1. **"Maybe I'm Amazed"**

   Baby, I'm amazed at the way you love me all the time

   According to *Rolling Stone* this song ranks as McCartney's top solo song. Its official music video has 7.4 million views, over 101 thousand likes, and zero dislikes. The fact that the video has that many views and nobody has disliked it speaks volumes about the song's popularity.

The most amazing thing about good teammates is their unwavering love for their team. They do indeed love their team all the time.

2. "Live and Let Die"

When you got a job to do you got to do it well

This song served as the theme to the James Bond film of the same name (Roger Moore's debut as 007). McCartney wrote the lyrics but only allowed producers to use the song if they agreed to use the version recorded by his band, Wings.

Good teammates are committed to doing their job. Regardless of what role they're assigned, they insist on doing their job to the absolute best of their abilities.

3. "Here Comes the Sun"

Here comes the Sun and I say, It's all right

From the Beatles' Grammy-winning *Abby Road* album, "Here Comes the Sun" was written by bandmate George Harrison about the unpleasantness of long, cold English winters. McCartney played bass and provided back-up vocals during the famous recording.

Good teammates provide their teams with hope. Their arrival calms our spirits, warms our souls, and lets us know everything is going to be all right with the same daily consistency as the rising sun.

4. "Hey Jude"

Take a sad song and make it better
Remember to let her into your heart
Then you can start to make it better

This song was the Beatles' most successful single in the USA. McCartney wrote it to comfort John Lennon's son, Julian, after Lennon divorced the boy's mother, Cynthia Powell, for Yoko Ono. Many fans view "Hey Jude" as the ultimate comfort song.

Good teammates are empathetic. They have a way of comforting us when we are sad. But good teammates are also invested. They start to make their teams' problems better when they become invested enough to let others' problems into their hearts.

5. "Let It Be"

When I find myself in times of trouble
Mother Mary comes to me
Speaking words of wisdom
Let it be

"Let It Be" was the last song released on the last Beatles album before McCartney revealed that he was leaving the band. Some have speculated that the "Mother Mary" lyric is a reference to the Virgin Mary. Others have speculated it's a tribute to McCartney's late mother, whose name was Mary.

But former Beatles roadie, personal assistant, and general righthand man, Mal (Malcolm) Evans claimed in a television special that the original lyric was "When I find myself in times of trouble, Brother Malcolm comes to me" and that he was the song's inspiration.

During our greatest moments of doubt, good teammates provide us with reassurance. They speak words of wisdom that remind us to focus on what we can control and not fret over what we cannot.

6. "Come Together"

Come together, right now, over me

With mentions of "old flat top," "ju-ju eyeball," "toe-jam football," and "monkey fingers," the lyrics to this song are bizarre, if not mismatched, by any standard. Yet when accompanied by music, they "come together" to form sheer genius.

The most successful teams are an eclectic collection of personalities that come together in pursuit of a common purpose. The only "good teammate" improvement I would make to this song is to alter the lyrics to be: "Come together, right now, put we over me."

7. "All You Need Is Love"

All you need is love, love
Love is all you need

The Beatles played this song for the first time during a worldwide television special known as "Our World." The special was broadcast in 24 countries across six continents. The band was tasked with writing a song that would speak to people from all nations.

McCartney and Lennon were fans of songs with slogans that moved the masses. "All You Need is Love" became an anthem to the anti-war movement and 1967's "Summer of Love.'

Good teammates are fueled by their love for their team. Want to be a good teammate? All you need is love. No other special talents are required.

8. "With a Little Help from My Friends"

Oh, I get by with a little help from my friends
Mm, gonna try with a little help from my friends

From the Beatles' *Sgt. Pepper's Lonely Hearts Club Band* album, this song was written by John Lennon and Paul McCartney but sung by drummer Ringo Starr. Legend has it that Starr, who traditionally only played instruments, was nervous about singing.

However, he was able to make it through the experience with "a little help" from his friends.

Good teammates empower us to believe in ourselves. They give us the confidence to tackle challenges we might otherwise fear to be too difficult. No greater safety net exists than knowing you've got the support of a good teammate.

As always…Good teammates care. Good teammates share. Good teammates listen. Go be a good teammate.

The Curious Case of Good Teammates
JUNE 28

Curiosity is an important component of being a good teammate. People are quick to associate compliance and conformity with good teammates. But in my experience, curiosity has a greater influence on team success than either of those entities.

Curiosity leads to awareness. Consider what disrupts your team's culture. The most disruptive behaviors are usually rooted in a lack of awareness. Team members don't realize how their habits annoy those around them. They fail to recognize what they're not good at. They don't know about their blind spots.

Regardless of whether those issues are the result of ignorance or arrogance, they cause unnecessary drama on teams that manifests in relationship friction, diminished synergy, and members not being as impactful as they could be.

Drama erodes a team's culture more than errant compliance or deficient conformity combined.

Organizational psychologist Tasha Eurich found that 95% of people think they're self-aware, but less than 15% actually are. In her book *Insight*, Eurich cites a primary reason for this disconnect to be what she calls the "cult of self" (the self-absorbed, "feel good" effect brought on by social media that makes people happier when they see themselves in a more positive light).

In other words, we've become conditioned to not want to acknowledge our flaws.

Good teammates are not content to accept the allure of the "cult of self." They strive to develop a "curiosity of self" that compels them to wonder about the answers to questions like: *What habits do I have that annoy others? What am I not good at? What are my blind spots?*

Curiosity leads to progress. If team members only focus on maintaining the status quo, they'll plateau and eventually become obsolete. For teams to stay on top, they must discover new methodologies and be receptive to exploring alternative strategies.

By being curious about what else they can do or how they can do "it" better, team members ward off stagnation and create opportunities for growth.

Curiosity leads to preparedness. All teams are bound to contend with unexpected challenges. What happens if an essential team member gets injured, falls ill, or becomes otherwise incapacitated? How should those situations be handled?

Research has shown that preparedness starts when teams are "collectively curious about anomalies" that could derail their development. By identifying potential challenges before they materialize, good teammates minimize the damage brought on by misfortune.

Compliance and conformity set teams up for success. But curiosity about disruptions, innovations, and unexpected challenges make teams successful.

As always…Good teammates care. Good teammates share. Good teammates listen. Go be a good teammate.

The research referenced above can be found at https://www.emerald.com/insight/ content/doi/10.1108/SL-05-2022-0051/full/html

Insist on the Rise, Resist the Pull
JULY 5

I received an email this week from a mother seeking advice on a problem her son was having with his teammates.

Her son, Tyler, was the best player on his baseball team. She said he was naturally gifted but also "extremely dedicated." Tyler had made considerable sacrifices to develop his skills that other members of his team had not.

After being named the MVP of a recent tournament, his fifth such award of the season, Tyler overheard some unsettling comments in the dugout:

> *Shocker! Tyler got MVP.*
> *How many awards is Tyler going to get?*
> *Tyler wins everything.*
> *They might as well rename it the Tyler Award.*
> *Big surprise, they gave Tyler another award.*

It wasn't only the words that bothered Tyler, it was also their accompanying tone and the spirit in which they were said.

Tyler felt that he had performed well enough to receive the recognition, but his teammates' response caused him to be resentful of the attention.

Tyler's teammates were jealous, envious, emotional, and—intentionally or unintentionally—they were creating a toxic environment that made him want to cower to appeasement.

His mother was adamant that she didn't want Tyler to back off or "dummy himself down" to fit in. She worried, however, that if she didn't provide Tyler with some guidance, that is exactly the approach he would take.

I have seen similar situations occur in other team settings. In the workplace, for instance, I have seen employees resent colleagues who show up early, stay late, and go above and beyond the call of duty. Instead of respecting and appreciating the effort, those employees feel ill will when their more dedicated colleagues get promotions.

Mismanaging that *ill-will* will eventually tear a team apart.

High achievers make poor teammates feel uncomfortable. The most toxic teammates I know despise having to rise to the level of their high achieving teammates. They would much rather remain comfortable and pull high achieving teammates down to their level.

Good teammates insist on the rise and resist the pull. My advice to Tyler and anyone in this situation is twofold:

1. Always be the hardest worker on your team.
2. Always be the kindest person on your team.

Much of what Tyler was feeling was beyond his control. He couldn't control what awards he was given any more than he could control how others felt about him receiving those awards. Tyler needed to focus on what he could control—his effort and his attitude.

By always being the hardest worker on your team, you legitimize your accolades. You make it difficult for people to question your worthiness. Moreover, you create a sense of inner peace for yourself that allows you to feel at ease with positive recognition.

You worked hard and know in your heart that you earned whatever attention you receive.

By always being the kindest person on your team, you prevent yourself from appearing entitled. Kindness allows you to accept awards with graciousness, appear thankful for your blessings, demonstrate character, and show appreciation to those who contributed to your success.

Kindness endears because it isn't about how others treat you, it's about how you treat others *regardless* of how they treat you.

Any high achiever who backs off or dummies down their efforts to appease their teammates does their team a disservice. Good teammates refuse to take that approach because they know doing so isn't what's best for their team.

Good teammates understand that when one of us wins we all win. That knowledge allows them to accept their achievements as well as their teammates' achievements.

As always...Good teammates care. Good teammates share. Good teammates listen. Go be a good teammate.

Gallantry in Action
JULY 12

Today's meanderings come from the *On This Date in History* files. On July 12, 1862, President Abraham Lincoln signed into legislation a measure that created the United States Army's highest and most prestigious award for military valor—the Medal of Honor.

According to the Congressional Medal of Honor Society, a total of 3,534 medals have been awarded since the decoration's creation. While the criteria has evolved over the years, the Medal of Honor has always retained an association with actions that go above and beyond the call of duty.

The wording in Lincoln's original measure called for the Medal of Honor to be bestowed upon those who distinguished themselves through "gallantry in action" during times of insurrection.

I like the phrase "gallantry in action" because the concept applies to the art of being a good teammate. Good teammates

45

are frequently called to exhibit gallantry (courageousness, bravery) in their actions.

They're gallant whenever they do what's right instead of what's popular. They're gallant whenever they confront the wayward behaviors of toxic teammates. They're gallant whenever they choose selflessness over selfishness.

Though these actions may not share the same dangers as those on the battlefield, they do come with their own relative level of risk.

Doing what's right instead of what's popular might get you laughed at. Confronting a toxic teammate might get you shunned. Choosing selflessness over selfishness might get you thought a fool.

Willie Johnson, the youngest person to have ever been awarded the Medal of Honor, was just eleven years old when he enlisted in the Union Army. He served as a drummer boy in Company D of the Vermont Third Infantry.

Having drummers on the battlefield seems silly by contemporary standards. But in the days prior to radios, satellites, and cell phones, musicians played a vital role in infantry communications.

Under the orders of General George McClellan, Johnson's unit was forced to retreat during the arduous Seven Days Battle on the Virginia Peninsula. With Confederates in pursuit, many of the fleeing soldiers discarded their equipment to "hasten" their retreat—an act viewed at the time as selfish and cowardly.

Johnson, however, never abandoned his drum nor his responsibilities. Tales of his bravery soon made their way to

President Lincoln's desk. Lincoln awarded Johnson the Medal of Honor shortly thereafter.

An article in the St. Johnsbury *Caledonian,* Johnson's hometown newspaper, quoted text from Lincoln's citation that distinguished the boy as "being the only drummer who brought his drum from the field." Johnson's story highlights two important elements of gallantry and its relationship to teamwork.

If your team is struggling, consider the following:

1. In moments of peril, do members of your team revert to self-preservation? Do they abandon their commitment to their team to save themselves? Or do they engage in "gallantry in action?"

2. How is "gallantry in action" honored on your team? Are medals awarded? Is it recognized through some other meaningful way? Or is it treated as unceremonious behavior?

Successful teams encourage, embrace, and reward gallantry. By doing so, they create a culture capable of withstanding the most difficult challenges.

As always…Good teammates care. Good teammates share. Good teammates listen. Go be a good teammate.

National Be a Good Teammate Day
JULY 19

The two most anticipated days in a child's life are usually Christmas and that child's birthday. Unfortunately for some children, those two occasions happen to occur at the same time.

I was born a "Christmas baby" and can personally attest to the frustration of having to share your birthday with a major holiday.

Receiving a *Christmas/birthday* gift from a relative or having my birthday present wrapped in Christmas paper always left me feeling slighted. As did never being able to bring cupcakes to school to celebrate with my classmates or have sleepovers *on* my actual birth date.

When I got older, I came to understand why Christmas birthdays are challenging for families. Finances are tighter, time is more finite, and logistics are a nightmare. Christmas birthdays amplify the stress of the holiday season.

But just because I understood the issue, didn't mean I stopped feeling slighted. One day my girlfriend—who eventually became my wife—suggested that I compensate for being "cheated" by picking an alternative date to celebrate what she called "Lance Day."

Her suggestion seemed like a good idea, so I picked the date of July 22 for *my* day. No other holiday fell on that date and it was spaced far enough away from Christmas to provide reprieve. The numerical date (7/22) also coincided with my high school football number (7) and my high school basketball number (22), which made it easy to remember.

I enjoyed celebrating "Lance Day" over the years. But the more I immersed myself into the art of being a good teammate, the less happy I became about the occasion's premise. I grew to want the date to be associated with something bigger than myself.

Last year, I successfully submitted for July 22 to be officially recognized as "National Be a Good Teammate Day."

Good teammates make being part of the team worthwhile. They help us when we're struggling, congratulate us when we're succeeding, and encourage us while we're striving. National Be a Good Teammate Day recognizes the sacrifices, kindness, and generosity of these selfless individuals.

Whether it's sports, family, community, school, or work, everybody is part of a team. Use this date to show your appreciation to those willing to put the needs of their "team" ahead of themselves.

On National Be a Good Teammate Day, make an extra effort to express your gratitude to team members who go above and beyond the call of duty. Honor their contributions to the team with a boisterous "Thank you!" or a well-deserved high five or hug.

Here are some additional ways to celebrate:

- Make an unsolicited *good teammate move* for someone on your team
- Take a teammate to lunch
- Gift a teammate a copy of *The WE Gear* book
- Write a handwritten note letting a teammate know what specifically you appreciate about them
- Reconnect with a former teammate and reminisce about fun times of the past
- Share a photo of you and a teammate on social media and use the hashtag *#NationalBeAGoodTeammateDay*

One final note...

If you are the type of teammate whose selflessness and kindness goes unrecognized, reward yourself on July 22 with a slice of *victory cake*. You've earned it!

As always…Good teammates care. Good teammates share. Good teammates listen. Go be a good teammate.

The above reference to "Victory Cake" comes from Chapter 14 in Teammate Tuesdays. Victory cake is a celebratory way to ward of jealousy and reinforce the concept that "when one of us wins, we all win."

Ketchup Teammates
JULY 26

A post on my community's Facebook page asked which local restaurant has the best French fries. The post garnered a surprisingly large and enthusiastic response.

The replies varied from fast food giants like McDonalds and Chick-Fil-A to some of the smaller, quainter, hometown eateries. As I scrolled through the comments, one thing became increasingly clear to me: People sure are passionate about their French fries!

Some insisted that only thin-cut fries merited consideration. Others argued that thin-cut fries, by definition, were inferior to thick-cut fries. The waffle fry contingency scoffed at both assertions.

According to *National Geographic*, the average American eats almost 30 pounds of French fries per year. The *Daily Mirror* reports that a typical Brit gobbles more than twice that amount annually.

In full disclosure, I too am passionate about French fries. I love all varieties and can't say that I disagreed with any of the submissions to the community Facebook post. They were all worthy of consideration.

What's interesting about French fries is that individually a case could be made for any style being the best. But if you were to mix styles together, they wouldn't be nearly as good.

For instance, a bite consisting of a handful of McDonald's thin-cut fries could be tasty. But a bite consisting of a McDonald's thin-cut fry, a Chick-Fil-A waffle fry, and a Red Robin's thick-cut tavern fry wouldn't taste right.

The different textures and seasonings aren't complimentary to each other—*unless* they're all dipped in ketchup. Ketchup is the great bonding agent. It neutralizes the varying textures and gives the bite a consistent flavor. Essentially, ketchup brings the bite together.

On teams, *ketchup teammates* serve a similar purpose.

Assembling the most talented individuals won't automatically lead to team success. Teams need members who are willing and able to shed their individual egos, sacrifice for the greater good, provide support, and abandon personal agendas.

Ketchup teammates don't necessarily possess the most desired physical talents. Their value to the team isn't tied to those distinctions. Their value is found in their complimentary talents, like their willingness to assume less heralded roles and their capacity to simply *get along* with everyone on the team.

It's easy to become enamored with an individual's physical talents, much in the same way that it's easy to become enamored with a particular style of French fries. But unlike a basket of French fries, teams aren't homogeneous. They're an assembly of individuals with different backgrounds and varying talents.

Don't discount the value of ketchup teammates. Their contributions hold the team together and make team success possible.

As always…Good teammates care. Good teammates share. Good teammates listen. Go be a good teammate.

*The National Geographic statistic referenced above is from Rubb, Rebecca. "Are French Fries Truly French?" January 8, 2015. https://www.nationalgeographic.com/culture/article/are-french-fries-truly-french

**The Daily Mirror report referenced above is from Alexander, Stian. "Brits Gobble Five Stone of Chips Every Year as Yorkshire Folk Top List of Spud Fans." July 15, 2022. https://www.mirror.co.uk/news/uk-news/brits-gobble-five-stone-chips-27493701

Ten Ways Good Teammates Start a New Season
AUGUST 2

Starting a new season can be both exhilarating and stressful. The unwritten slate holds hope for positive outcomes, yet the unknown is always accompanied by anxiety.

Teams that get off to a good start tend to increase their chances of having successful seasons. Good teammates take deliberate measures to put their teams in a position to succeed—especially at the start of the season.

With the impending start of a new academic year, here are ten ways you can start a new season like a good teammate:

1. **Let go of past successes.** What you accomplished last season has no bearing on what you will achieve this season. You are now part of a new team, facing new challenges. Complacently basking in former glory won't bring you future success.

2. **Remember past missteps.** Recognizing last season's mistakes *and* committing to not making the same mistakes again leads to progress.

3. **Share what you learned during the offseason.** What did you discover during your time away from your teammates that can help them become better versions of themselves? Don't selfishly keep this information to yourself.

4. **Be receptive to new ideas.** What new training methods or strategies have other members of your team discovered during their time away from you? Don't be stubborn or too set in your ways to be open to change.

5. **Evaluate your habits.** What do you want to be known for? You are ultimately a product of your habits. The start of a new season is the perfect time to abandon bad habits and adopt beneficial habits.

6. **Be organized.** Time is usually at a premium during the start of any season. There's a lot to be done in a limited number of hours. Being organized leads to efficiency and maximizes the time you have available.

7. **Integrate new teammates.** What can you do to help welcome the newest additions to your team? Jelled teams become productive teams.

8. **Align with team leadership.** See it as your responsibility to find out what your team leaders' goals and priorities are for the new season. Once you understand their expectations, position yourself to facilitate their vision.

9. **Expect *unexpected* challenges.** People fail when they fail to prepare. Unexpected challenges (e.g., injuries, illnesses, additions, departures, etc.) will inevitably pop up during the season. You reduce the extent of these disruptions by expecting them and having contingency plans in place.

10. **Observe your fellow teammates.** Keep an eye out for straggling teammates, as well as those who are exceeding expectations. Encourage the ones falling behind. Praise the ones who are getting ahead.

How you start the season might not matter as much as how you finish, but getting off to a good start makes the probability of a good finish far more likely.

As always…Good teammates care. Good teammates share. Good teammates listen. Go be a good teammate.

Embracing a Team Ego
AUGUST 9

I was saddened by Bill Russell's recent passing. He was an inspiring figure whose example impacted countless lives. He was also the source of a good teammate insight that I hold incredibly dear.

On the basketball court, Russell's accomplishments were plenty: five NBA most valuable player awards, 12 All-Star selections, an Olympic gold medal, a 55-game college winning streak, two NCAA championships, and 11 NBA titles.

Russell co-authored two of my all-time favorite books, *Red and Me* and *Russell Rules*. Both books mention the Hall of Famer's unique perspective on ego—a perspective that I've found to be shared by many good teammates.

In Chapter Two of *Russell Rules*, Russell discusses a talk he gave about ego to the 1999 Boston Celtics, who were in the middle of a nine-game losing streak and not playing as a unit:

"I began by telling (the Celtics players) that despite that so much had been written about me being the most unselfish player, I was the most egotistical player they would ever meet. All kinds of nervous smiles were coming back at me from people who were not sure what was coming next. These smiles disappeared when I said, 'Do you know the difference between your ego and mine? My ego is not a personal ego, it's a team ego. My ego demands—for myself—the success of my team. My personal achievement became my team achievement.'"

Ego is your opinion of yourself, especially your feeling of worth in terms of your own importance and ability.

Being egotistical (excessively conceited, self-absorbed, or self-centered) is generally viewed as detrimental to team culture. But that isn't necessarily the case with team members who have a "team ego."

Personal egos come from statistics like points, rebounds, and assists. Team egos come from the final score.

Personal egos cause you to be reluctant to do work that you think is beneath you. Team egos compel you to do whatever is necessary for your team to succeed.

Personal egos start with "I." Team egos start with "We."

Some of the most impactful teammates I have ever encountered had a swagger rooted in their team ego. They projected brash confidence and took pride in their teams' accomplishments without any allusion to their individual accomplishments.

How they carried themselves did not rub the other members of their teams the wrong way. In fact, their swagger inspired the other members to also embrace a team ego.

Sports Illustrated called Russell sports' "greatest winner." But limiting the summation of Russell's legacy to his on-court accomplishments would be a travesty. He championed social injustice throughout his life and used his platform to make the world a better place. His willingness to engage in causes that did not directly affect him sprung from his team ego.

Embracing your team ego will undoubtedly lead you to do the same.

As always…Good teammates care. Good teammates share. Good teammates listen. Go be a good teammate.

*The Sports Illustrated *article referenced above is from McCallum, Jack. "Remembering Bill Russell: The Greatest Winner in Sports." July 31, 2022. https://www.si.com/nba/2022/07/31/bill-russell-death-boston-celtics-obituary*

Values That Devalue
AUGUST 16

A friend was venting to me about his son's lack of playing time. He described how his son was clearly one of the fastest, most talented players on the field, yet the coaches weren't playing him in the games. He was adamant that his son deserved a bigger role on the team.

I listened to everything my friend had to say, and, frankly, he seemed to have some valid complaints. At his insistence, I agreed to go and watch his son's next practice and let him know what I thought.

What I observed and reported back to my friend was enlightening—but not in the way he had anticipated.

Practice began with the players warming up with a set of basic calisthenics. They were supposed to do ten repetitions of each exercise. My friend's son never did more than seven or eight and he never counted aloud with the rest of the team.

When the team ran drills, my friend's son talked back to coaches anytime they tried to correct his technique.

During scrimmages, my friend's son excelled. He dominated on the field and wasn't shy about boasting about his achievement whenever he scored. I found it interesting, however, that he never celebrated when one of his teammates scored. His excitement was limited exclusively to his own achievements.

At the end of practice, the coaches gathered the team for conditioning. My friend's son didn't bother to touch the lines when he ran his sprints.

When practice finally concluded, my friend's son, as I had anticipated, left the field without helping to carry any equipment or clean up the bench area.

My friend was right in that his son was one of the fastest, most talented players on the team. That fact was evident to me. Why he wasn't getting more playing time was also evident: His values *devalued* his value to the team.

Your values set the parameters of your value to your team. Good values (loyalty, honesty, integrity, etc.) make you of greater value because they influence team success.

In the case of my friend's son, the values conveyed during practice were selfishness, pretentiousness, and entitlement. Who would entrust playing time to someone who had those values?

Talent isn't the only element that defines worth. My friend was angry at his son's coaches for not playing his son more. He should've instead been grateful for them holding his son accountable and teaching him to become a better teammate.

Players with bad values inevitably grow up to become employees with bad values. Selfish, pretentious, entitled employees are a primary source of workplace dysfunction.

If someone you know is feeling undervalued on their team, take a deep look at the values they are espousing. Perhaps it's their values that are devaluing their worth.

As always…Good teammates care. Good teammates share. Good teammates listen. Go be a good teammate.

The Need for Bellringers
AUGUST 23

Are you a *bellringer*?

Yesterday, I experienced a poor customer service situation at a big box home improvement store.

Despite having multiple checkout lanes, the store only had two registers open. One was a temperamental self-checkout whose error light was constantly blinking and the other was manned by a large, surly employee whose movement mirrored that of a snail.

As I stood in a long, winding line of angry patrons, it became clear that the issue wasn't due to a lack of staffing. I saw plenty of employees standing around chatting with each other. I even saw a pair of managers stroll by and joke with those employees.

None of them seemed bothered by the long checkout lines or concerned about their customers' frustrations.

The greatest of all disrespect is the disregard of another's time. What I encountered at that store was a complete disregard for my and the other customers' time. The employees' inattention created a customer service failure void of empathy, decency, and respect.

On my way out of the store, I noticed a sign encouraging customers to ring an adjacent bell if they received great service. The improbability of that happening caused me to laugh out loud. Another customer saw me looking at the sign and snarked: "Not a lot of *bellringers* in this place today."

I understood what he meant.

Bellringers are important. And the concept applies to more than customer service, too. Bellringers play a vital part in team success.

Here are three types of bellringers that every team needs:

Bellringer #1: Those who ring the bell to share good news. As suggested above, a job well done deserves acknowledgement. This type of bellringer appreciates and celebrates their teammates' contributions, and their doing so sparks virality.

Bellringer #2: Those who ring the bell to warn of danger. In the days of yore, villagers would ring church bells to warn others of approaching danger, like invaders, fires, or tornadoes. By sounding an alarm, this type of bellringer steers their team clear of toxicity, ethical violations, and other destructive behaviors.

Bellringer #3: Those who ring the bell to initiate change. In collision sports, such as football or hockey, announcers often say a participant "got his bell rung," meaning another player hit that participant exceptionally hard. Sometimes, stagnant, apathetic teams need someone who will shake things up. This type of bellringer possesses the courage and charisma to initiate change.

Just like being a good teammate, being a bellringer requires no special physical talent. Anyone with a desire to serve the needs of their team can assume this role. If your team has good news to share, is in danger, or needs to initiate change, don't hesitate to grasp the rope and ring the bell.

As always…Good teammates care. Good teammates share. Good teammates listen. Go be a good teammate.

Don't Panic
AUGUST 30

In exploring the art of being a good teammate, one of the most fascinating elements I've observed is how rarely good teammates panic.

To clarify, good teammates encounter anxiety the same as everyone else. Their lives are not void of stressful events. They contend with fear, apprehension, and the gamut of stressors, yet they possess an uncanny ability to not panic during these encounters.

The American Psychological Association explains anxiety "as an emotion characterized by feelings of tension and worry that stem from an individual anticipating impending danger or misfortune."

Anxiety is a natural human response to the real or perceived presence of threat. Who hasn't experienced pins and needles, a churning in their stomach, or an increased heart rate when stressed?

Panic, on the other hand, is a sudden, intense reaction involving terror, confusion, and irrational behavior. In layman's terms, panic happens when individuals lose mental control over the moment.

I have yet to ascertain *why* good teammates project a quiet confidence when others panic. Is it because they are more comfortable with their role? Is it because they're more prepared? Is because they're more action oriented?

Is it a combination of all those things? Probably. What I have noticed is that good teammates tend to employ several strategies that keep them from panicking:

1. **They set damage parameters.** Good teammates immediately establish what the ideal resolution would be and what the worst-case scenario could be. Then, they accept both premises without obsessing over either. Imagine losing your phone at the store. The best case scenario would be a kind customer found it and turned it into customer service. The worst case scenario would be someone took it and you have to buy an new one. Both scenarios are manageable. The stress of the unknown can be paralyzing. By setting parameters, good teammates contain the unknown. They recognize the ends of the spectrum and realize that they are capable of handling wherever the outcome falls on that spectrum.

2. **They focus on solutions instead of reactions.** Panic often comes from fixating on less urgent questions.

How did this happen? Who's to blame? What will others think when they find out? In the preceding example, rather than focusing on how your phone got lost, who caused you to be distracted, or why you were rushed to leave the store, concentrate on what needs to be done to solve the issue—like finding someone to call your phone, activating your lost phone mode, or calling your phone carrier. There will be a time to analyze what when wrong and who might be to blame, but that time doesn't have to be the present juncture.

3. **They break down the issue into smaller, more manageable problems.** Good teammates choose to view the big problem as nothing more than a series of small, solvable problems. For instance, you need to: (a) Determine if your phone is lost or stolen, (b) Activate your Find-My-Phone app, (c) Contact your phone carrier, and (d) Let your family know you don't have access to your phone in case there's an emergency. This approach causes the bigger, seemingly overwhelming problem to become far less daunting because all those tasks are achievable.

Panic can be debilitating for individuals and disastrous for teams. By utilizing these strategies good teammates keep their anxiety from spiraling into panic.

As always…Good teammates care. Good teammates share. Good teammates listen. Go be a good teammate.

When Parents Are Good Teammates
SEPTEMBER 6

Seeing their child struggle can be frustrating for parents, especially sports parents. Maybe the child is unhappy with their playing time or their role. Maybe they're upset with something hurtful their coach said. Or, maybe they're disappointed with how they're playing.

It's important for parents to adopt a good teammate mindset during these moments because the wrong response can have a lasting effect on their child's mental well-being.

Here are three tips for sports parents dealing with an athlete who's struggling:

1. **Don't try to solve the problem for them.** Instead, lead them to solve their own problem. You can help them do this by asking open ended questions like: *Why do you think that is? How do you think you could change that? What do you think would happen if you tried _____?*

Sports are a vehicle for teaching life skills. This approach will teach your child important problem-solving skills and empower them with the confidence to handle adversity.

It's ok to remain on the periphery and use your experience to guide the conversation, but don't monopolize it. And remember, the best open-ended question is often: What are you learning from this?

2. **Don't disrespect the opinion.** A coach's comments can sting, particularly if they're delivered with an insensitive tone.

I'm not referring to comments that are illegal, immoral, or otherwise cross a line. I mean comments related to your child's ability. For instance, the coach tells your child they're too slow or not good enough to play a certain position.

Whenever your child shares this information with you, don't disrespect the opinion. Make it clear to your child that the coach is entitled their opinion and reaffirm that what the coach said was exactly that—their opinion.

Neither you nor your child are required to agree with the coach's opinion. You can dismiss it without being disrespectful. If you react contemptuously, you'll undermine the coach's authority and taint the respect your child should be developing for persons in authority.

3. **Don't critique their performance right after the game.** This may seem like an opportune time to share your thoughts, but doing so can make the car ride home a traumatizing experience for your child.

Resist the urge to provide feedback about their play or the outcome of the game. Whether they won, lost, played well or poorly, simply tell your child: "I enjoyed watching you and your teammates play."

Consistently providing this response will keep your child from attaching their worth to the game's outcome or their statistics. You can convey more in-depth feedback later, once the emotional dust settles and they're in a less vulnerable state. (*By the way, the addendum "and your teammates" is crucial to conveying the admiration you have for them being part of a team.)

Speaking of car rides, I had a parent—who happened to also be a respected family therapist—tell me that a "*looooonnng* car ride" can be the best therapy for kids who are reluctant to tell their parents what's bothering them. Just keep patiently driving. They'll eventually start talking. And when they do, be a good teammate and listen.

As always…Good teammates care. Good teammates share. Good teammates listen. Go be a good teammate.

Lessons Learned From Service Animals
SEPTEMBER 13

I took my family to see the movie *Gigi & Nate*. My daughters loved the movie, and so did I. It's loaded with examples of impactful good teammates moves.

Inspired by true events, the movie tells the story of the relationship between Nate, a despondent 22-year-old paraplegic, and his unusual service animal, Gigi, a precocious capuchin monkey.

Gigi and Nate is based on the book *Kasey to the Rescue: The Remarkable Story of a Monkey and a Miracle* that Ellen Rogers wrote about her paraplegic son, Ned Sullivan.

The movie takes a few creative liberties with Rogers' book, like changing the monkey's name and the cause of her son's paralysis. Rogers' son was paralyzed from a car accident. The character in the movie was paralyzed from meningitis.

However, the movie holds true in depicting the incredible connection her son had with his service animal and how greatly that animal improved his life.

Service animals are amazing creatures. They can assist with mobility issues, open and close doors, and pick up dropped objects. They can also alert to dangers and recognize the onset of medical emergencies such as seizures or low blood sugar.

On top of all of that, service animals can provide comfort and companionship. A study from Purdue University's College of Veterinary Medicine shows that service animals have a positive and distinctly measurable effect on their human's psychosocial health.

Service animals embody the spirit of what it means to be a good teammate because, as their name points out, they serve. They purposefully attend to the needs of their human.

Similarly, good teammates *purposefully* attend to the needs of their team.

Service requires commitment, humility, and drive. To serve effectively, you must be willing to suppress ego and forego convenience. You must be motivated by more than personal benefit. Your duty must become your honor.

The miracle is that none of these *requirements* are beyond any of us. As Dr. Martin Luther King said, "Everybody can be great, because anybody can serve."

An interesting side note to my family's excursion to see *Gigi & Nate*: Near the end of the movie, my daughters started giggling and excitedly pointing at something in the theater. While I was trying to figure out what was drawing their attention, a capuchin monkey crawled across the seatbacks in front of me. It belonged to another person watching the movie, who graciously introduced her service monkey to my daughters when we exited the theater.

Seeing how excited that monkey made my daughters reminded me of another important good teammate trait of service animals: Their presence evokes positive emotions in those with whom they encounter.

As always…Good teammates care. Good teammates share. Good teammates listen. Go be a good teammate.

Johnny Appleseed's Strategy
SEPTEMBER 20

Johnny Appleseed is among history's most beloved folk heroes—and arguably its most eccentric. By choice, he walked barefoot, clothed himself in a burlap sack, donned a tin pot for a hat, and, of course, planted apple trees across the American frontier.

A lot of people are surprised to learn that Johnny Appleseed was in fact a real person. John Chapman earned the nickname "Johnny Appleseed" because of his penchant for carrying a leather bag filled with apple seeds.

Like many folk heroes, much of Chapman's life has been fictionalized through film and literature. The notion of him randomly spreading his seeds wherever he went falls into this category. The truth is a bit more pragmatic.

Apples were an important part of frontier life. They were a source of food for families and livestock. But even more so, they were the source of the frontier's beverage of choice— hard cider.

Additionally, homestead agreements required landowners to, among other things, plant 50 apples trees on their property in order to secure permanent land rights.

Chapman was a savvy opportunist, adept at predicting the direction of the frontier movement. He would advance ahead of the settlers and plant apple orchards. He would then sell these trees to settlers when they arrived.

To be successful in this endeavor, Chapman had to be strategic in where he chose to plant his orchards, ergo, there was nothing *random* about his seed spreading.

Spread probably isn't a word most of us associate with the art of being a good teammate. But it should be because that's what good teammates do best. They spread (e.g., energy, enthusiasm, hope, kindness, goodwill, etc.).

In my book *The WE Gear*, I refer to this quality as being viral.

When it comes to virality, good teammates should follow Johnny Appleseed's example and be strategic in when, where and how they spread. Some situations are best served by exuberance, others by temperance. Before you go guns blazing, consider the timing, location, and delivery of your actions.

Next Monday is Johnny Appleseed Day. Use this occasion to *strategically* spread a little extra energy, enthusiasm, hope, and kindness on your team. Doing so will undoubtedly cause you to become as beloved as the holiday's namesake.

As always…Good teammates care. Good teammates share. Good teammates listen. Go be a good teammate.

Inform, Inspire, Inflame
SEPTEMBER 27

Two sisters were going to be late for soccer practice because the older sister wasn't ready to leave on time. As their mother drove them to the field, the younger sister looked out the car window and said, "Practice is starting now."

Her comment ignited a heated fight between the siblings. The girls' mother asked the younger sister, "Why would you say that?"

The younger sister replied, "I was just trying to inform her of the facts."

No. No, she wasn't. She was trying to *inflame* her.

Two brothers were riding home from a basketball tournament where the older brother had just been named to the all-tournament team. Holding his trophy, the older brother turned to the younger brother and said, "You could earn a trophy too, if you were a better shooter and played harder."

His comment ignited a heated fight between the siblings. The boys' father asked the older brother, "Why would you say that?"

The older brother replied, "I was just trying to inspire him with the facts."

No. No, he wasn't. He was trying to *inflame* him.

Passive aggressive comments made under the guise of informing or inspiring, when the real intent is to provoke an adverse reaction, sabotage relationships—regardless if the relationship is between siblings, spouses, coworkers, or teammates.

In the above example, the younger sister's comments were born of ill-intent. She wasn't trying to relay helpful information. Everyone in the car already knew they were running late for practice. Her intent was to agitate her sister. She wanted to make her sister angry.

The same is true for the brothers. The older brother wasn't trying to inspire his younger brother. He wanted to agitate his younger brother by making him jealous.

There are times when teammates need to communicate unpleasant news to inform or inspire. But using passive aggressive, backhanded words that inflame the situation isn't the way to accomplish this objective.

Good teammates are mindful of the purpose of their words, and their mindfulness is reflected in what they say as well as what they choose *not* to say.

Before you speak, consider the purpose of your words. Are they intended to inform or inspire? Or are they simply intended to inflame? If the latter is the reason, then forego the delivery.

Relatedly, if you happen to find yourself on the receiving end of inflaming, passive aggressive comments, know that you have the power to extinguish their purpose by being *aggressively passive*. Instead of allowing your response to add fuel to an unnecessary fire, remove your reaction from the equation by refusing to engage. Remember, he who angers you owns you.

As always...Good teammates care. Good teammates share. Good teammates listen. Go be a good teammate.

Twelve Movies That Promote the Art of Being a Good Teammate
OCTOBER 4

A coach reached out to me over the weekend, wondering if I had any recommendations for movies he could show to his team that promote the art of being a good teammate.

This coach has done The Good Teammate Factory online program with his team and continues to do an absolutely amazing job of ingraining the concept of being a good teammate into his team's culture.

He planned to invite the entire team over to his house to watch a movie on his lawn. The coach didn't want to show just any movie, though. He wanted to specifically show a movie that reinforced good teammate behaviors.

His goal was to assemble a selection of applicable movies and then have his senior captains pick the movie from that list. What a great idea!

Movies bond teams through shared emotion. They make teammates laugh, cry, and feel inspired. The experience has the power to influence team culture in a meaningful way.

I sent the coach a few suggestions but have been thinking about my reply ever since. It occurred to me that others may benefit from this information.

So today I'm sharing twelve movies, in no particular order, that promote the art of being a good teammate. (*Because good teammates share!)

1. *Hoosiers*

   Plot: A controversial coach leads the Hickory Huskers towards an Indiana High School State Championship. This movie's loaded with good teammate moves!

   Includes Examples Of: suppressing ego, standing up for others, and valuing synergy

   Key Quote: "One other thing. I play, coach stays. He goes, I go." –Jimmy Chitwood

2. *Cool Runnings*

   Plot: The improbable story of the first Jamaican Olympic bobsled team.

   Includes Examples Of: sacrifice, humility, and courage

   Key Quote: "We're different. People are always afraid of what's different." –Yul Brenner

3. *Invictus*

Plot: Nelson Mandela unites an apartheid-torn South Africa with the help of the Springbok rugby team.

Includes Examples Of: sacrifice and setting differences aside for the greater good

Key Quote: "You criticize without understanding. You seek only to address your own personal feelings. That is selfish thinking." –Nelson Mandela

4. *Pitch Perfect*

Plot: An eclectic all-girls singing group comes together to challenge their campus rival.

Includes Examples Of: virality, how influential energy can be in bringing out the best in others, and commitment

Key Quote: "Even though some of you are pretty thin, you all have fat hearts, and that's what matters." –Fat Amy

5. *Apollo 13*

Plot: NASA works to bring a crew safely back to Earth after their spacecraft is damaged.

Includes Examples Of: resiliency, trust, and being relentless when helping teammates in need

Key Quote: "I don't care about what anything was DESIGNED to do. I care about what it CAN do."
– Gene Kranz

6. *Rudy*

Plot: This movie is about an underdog individual pursuing his dream to be on the Notre Dame football team, but it's also about the many "good teammates" who help in this quest.

Includes Examples Of: dedication, gratitude, and recognizing others' contributions

Key Quote: "I want Rudy to dress in my place, coach. He deserves it." –Roland Steele

7. *The Great Escape*

Plot: (*An oldie but a goodie!) Allied prisoners plan an escape from a German POW camp during World War II.

Includes Examples Of: valuing roles, appreciating others' talents, and commitment to duty

Key Quote: "Colonel Von Luger, it is the sworn duty of all officers to try to escape. If they cannot escape, then it is their sworn duty to cause the enemy to use an inordinate number of troops to guard them."
–Ramsey

8. *Wonder*

   Plot: The heartwarming story of a boy with facial differences who attends mainstream school for the first time.

   Includes Examples Of: standing up for teammates who cannot stand up for themselves, seeing inner beauty, and ignoring outside opinions

   Key Quote: "Given the choice between being right and being kind, choose kind." –Summer

9. *Rise*

   Plot: Based on the real-life story of the Antetokounmpo family, Nigerian-Greek immigrants who became the first trio of brothers to become NBA champions.

   Includes Examples Of: sacrifice, perspective, empathy, and selfless drive

   Key Quote: "When one person in the family scores, the whole family scores." –Thanasis Antetokounmpo

10. *Coach Carter*

    Plot: An unconventional coach uses basketball to teach his players important life lessons that transcend the court.

Includes Examples Of: collective responsibility, holding each other accountable, and adaptation

Key Quote: "I'll do push-ups for him. You said we're a team. One person struggles, we all struggle. One player triumphs, we all triumph, right?" –Jason Lyle

11. *42*

Plot: The Brooklyn Dodgers' Jackie Robinson faces considerable challenges when he becomes the first African American to play in Major League Baseball.

Includes Examples Of: tolerance, compassion, courage, and trust

Key Quote: "Maybe tomorrow, we'll all wear 42, so nobody could tell us apart." –Pee Wee Reese

12. *Toy Story 2*

Plot: (An animated inclusion!) Woody, a cowboy doll, is stolen and his fellow toys go to great lengths to save him.

Includes Examples Of: determination, loyalty, and accepting the inconvenience of being invested

Key Quote: "We have a friend in need, and we will not rest until he's safe in Andy's room! Now, let's move out!" –Buzz Lightyear

What movies would you add to this list? Share your thoughts by sending an email to *info@coachloya.com*.

As always…Good teammates care. Good teammates share. Good teammates listen. Go be a good teammate.

Roosevelt's Absorbed Mindset
OCTOBER 11

Four U.S. presidents have been assassinated—John Kennedy, William McKinley, James Garfield, and Abraham Lincoln. Two others have had attempts made on their lives in which they were shot but only wounded—Ronald Reagan and Theodore Roosevelt.

This week in 1912, John Schrank tried to assassinate Roosevelt outside of a diner in Milwaukee, Wisconsin. Roosevelt wasn't the sitting president at the time of the attack.

He held the presidency from 1901-1909. Frustrated by the direction of the country, Roosevelt returned to politics and ran as a third-party candidate (the Progressive Party) in the 1912 election. He was on his way to deliver a campaign speech when Schrank shot him.

The bullet struck Roosevelt in the chest. But a reading glasses case and a folded copy of the speech in his jacket's inside pocket slowed the bullet's penetration, thereby saving his life.

An experienced soldier and hunter, Roosevelt quickly concluded that the bullet had not pierced his lungs since he was not coughing blood. Instead of going directly to the hospital, Roosevelt insisted that his driver take him to the auditorium where he was scheduled to speak.

A few minutes later, with the bullet still lodged in his chest, Roosevelt inspired the waiting audience with a near 90-minute speech titled "Progressive Cause Greater Than Any Individual."

How can such an extraordinary display of mental and physical toughness not be admired?

Roosevelt's example personified his speech's title. He took to the stage and began: "Friends, I shall ask you to be as quiet as possible. I don't know whether you fully understand that I have just been shot; but it takes more than that to kill a bull moose."

The "bull moose" comment became one of Roosevelt's most popular quotes. But something he said later in the speech epitomizes the mindset of a good teammate:

"I am in this cause with my whole heart and soul. I believe that the Progressive movement is for making life a little easier for all our people; a movement to try to take the burdens off the men and especially the women and children of this country. I am absorbed in the success of that movement."

Good teammates are fully committed. They pour their whole heart and soul into their teams. They care about the burdens of everyone on the team. And they are completely *absorbed* in their teams' success.

Too often, teams are derailed by members who are *self-absorbed* when they should be *team-absorbed*. Self-absorbed members allow individual agendas to overtake the best interests of their team.

Team-absorbed members accept that the teams' cause is greater than any individual on that team. This mindset allows them to experience higher levels of team success.

Not even a bull moose is strong enough to stop a team comprised of team-absorbed teammates.

As always...Good teammates care. Good teammates share. Good teammates listen. Go be a good teammate.

Your Happiest Hello
OCTOBER 18

Recently, I saw a sign hanging in an inmate's cell that caught my attention. The sign read: "I want to be your favorite hello and your hardest goodbye." My initial reaction was one of admiration. I felt inspired and thought, "That's powerful. That's a noble objective. That's something that we should all aspire to be."

Being a "favorite hello" means others look forward to your arrival. Your presence is appreciated and welcomed. Being a "hardest goodbye" means others hate to see you leave. They enjoy your company so much that your departure causes them sadness, perhaps even pain. Who wouldn't want to be thought of in these regards?

I decided in that instant that becoming people's favorite hello and hardest goodbye was going to be one of my life's new objectives. The more I thought about this endeavor, the more I began to question my initial reaction to the inmate's sign. Something about its wording wasn't sitting right.

It's easy to be someone's *favorite* hello. If I want to be my daughters' favorite hello, all I need to do is give them candy whenever they want. They will quickly come to *looooooove* seeing me!

But me always giving them something that isn't good for them is, well, *not* good for them. In the long run, my actions will rob them of happiness. I will contribute to their rotting teeth, malnutrition, and unhealthy habits. They will eventually resent my arrival.

During an intervention, I once heard the parent of an addict confess that she gives her teenage son money to get high because it "makes (her) life easier." She described how doing so keeps her son from incessantly nagging her or stealing from others.

The therapist running the intervention looked at the mother and posed a poignant question: "Over the years, has allowing your son to manipulate you like this made your life easier?"

When the mother thought about the totality of the situation, she responded with a heartfelt, "No."

To be truly noble, the endeavor needs to be changed from being someone's "favorite" hello to being their "happiest" hello. Favorite equates to pleasure, which is a short-term objective. Happiness is a far more impactful, eternal objective.

Being a happiest hello means your actions allow others to experience happiness.

Giving my daughters' all the candy they want will no doubt provide them with a dose of pleasure. But tempering how much I give them, teaching them healthy habits, and restraint will ultimately provide them with happiness—even if that reality isn't immediately realized.

Good teammates do not enable bad behaviors. They facilitate happiness. For that reason, they endeavor to be their fellow teammates' *happiest* hello.

As always…Good teammates care. Good teammates share. Good teammates listen. Go be a good teammate.

An Act of Grizzly Courage
OCTOBER 25

A grizzly bear attack near Cody, Wyoming last week is quickly becoming one of my all-time favorite good teammate move stories.

Brady Lowry and Kendell Cummings, sophomore teammates on the Northwest College wrestling team, were shed (antler) hunting in the Shoshone National Forest Saturday afternoon with a few other members of their team.

The pair were several miles from the trailhead entrance when a grizzly bear lunged from the brush, pinning Lowry to the ground. Lowry put up his arm to protect himself, but the bear's bite broke his arm. To try and free his teammate, Cummings jumped on the grizzly's back.

In case you happened to gloss over that last sentence, I'll repeat it for clarity and emphasis: **CUMMINGS JUMPED ON THE GRIZZLY'S BACK!**

"I had to get (the bear) off (Lowry). I had to do something. I couldn't watch my friend get torn up right in front of me," Cummings told KTVQ News.

Cummings proceeded to grab a fistful of the bear's fur and pull until the bear released Lowry.

The National Wildlife Federation describes the typical adult grizzly bear as weighing upwards of 700 pounds. I don't know exactly how much the bear Cummings jumped on weighed, but I do know that the Northwest Athletics website lists Cummings as wrestling at 141 pounds.

I am struggling to imagine a more courageous act of selfless bravery. GOOD. TEAMMATE. MOVE.

Sometimes, members of our team are being attacked by metaphorical grizzlies—behemoths taking the form of unkind words, unfair criticism, or unjust treatment. These occasions are when our teammates need us the most.

Are you courageous enough to *jump on the back* of a metaphorical grizzly attacking your teammate? Or are you immobilized by the fear of potential backlash or retaliation?

Cummings' actions were completely rooted in *The WE Gear*. He wasn't deterred by what could happen to him if he acted. He was consumed with doing what was best for his team in that moment—coming to his teammate's aid.

For the record, Cummings was subjected to *retaliation*. His actions caused him to actually suffer the worst of the incident. After he got the grizzly off Lowry, the bear turned and attacked him.

But a sequence of subsequent good teammate moves by other members of his party, a hunter in the area, a local farmer, and the Park County Search and Rescue team prevented this inspirational story from becoming one of tragedy.

Lowry and Cummings are expected to make a full recovery.

The beauty of courageous good teammate moves is that they often beget more courageousness. They empower others to get involved.

There's an old comedic (Me Gear) adage about escaping bear attacks: *You don't have to run faster than the bear to get away. You just have to run faster than the guy next to you.* I suspect Lowry and the rest of the Northwest College wrestling team are thankful Cummings chose not to embrace this selfish advice.

As always…Good teammates care. Good teammates share. Good teammates listen. Go be a good teammate.

The National Wildlife Federation statistic referenced above can be found at https://www.nwf.org/Educational-Resources/Wildlife-Guide/Mammals/Grizzly-Bear

Five Rules for Confronting Your Teammates
NOVEMBER 1

When your teammates' behaviors fall short of your teams' standards, *you* have an obligation to hold them accountable. Good teammates take this responsibility seriously.

Confronting wayward peers can be tricky business. They're not likely to appreciate your criticism, especially if you have no formal authority over them. *How* you approach the situation matters greatly. The wrong approach could cause them to become defensive or dismissive, which will exacerbate the problem.

Here are five rules good teammates follow for confronting their errant teammates:

1. **Never Criticize Before You Empathize**
   Why is your teammate acting the way that they are? Before you critique their behavior, make a point to try and understand the reason behind their actions. Are

they feeling underappreciated? Do they understand the expectations? Is there an ulterior agenda?

You won't be able to help them if you don't take the time to discover what's driving their waywardness.

2. **Give Them the Sweet, *Then* the Sour**

Begin your confrontation with a positive affirmation. Recognize something they're doing right before you bring up what they're doing wrong. For example: *Jesse, you're a hard worker. But your punctuality is disrupting our team. We need you to show up on time.*

Beginning the confrontation with blunt negativity will compel them to respond defensively. They will put up the proverbial wall and prevent your message from being transmitted.

3. **Attack the Action, Not the Actor**

Don't make your confrontation about the person, make it about their behavior. Avoid assigning labels. Instead of calling them *slow* or *lazy*, tell them: "You need to move faster" or "You need to be more active."

Karen Scheuer wrote a wonderful children's book about conflict resolution titled *A Bug and a Wish*. The concept is to confront offenders by stating: It bugs me when you _____. I wish you would _____. This simple script is an excellent way to keep the confrontation focused on the action instead of the actor.

4. **Steer Clear of Sarcasm**

   The word sarcasm comes from the ancient Greek word *sarkázein*, which meant "to tear flesh." Bitter, snarky remarks hurt and cue adverse reactions. Sarcastic comments may be funny to you and nearby onlookers, but they rarely are to the recipient.

   The objective of your confrontation should be to heal, not hurt. Forego the sarcasm in favor of more palatable phrasing.

5. **Control Your Temper**

   Confrontation involves an element of uncertainty. You don't know how the people you're confronting are going to react. They may embrace what you say. They may dismiss what you say. They may become defensive and launch an angering counterattack.

   You can't control their response, but you can control your response to their response. Remain calm and focus on the reason for the confrontation—to help your team move forward. Volatile, emotionally charged exchanges will not achieve this objective.

Adhering to these rules eases the difficulty associated with confrontation.

As always...Good teammates care. Good teammates share. Good teammates listen. Go be a good teammate.

The Centerfield Mindset
NOVEMBER 8

Saturday's World Series finale brought an end to Major League Baseball's season. During one of the broadcasts, I heard a commentator remark that the most frequently played song at MLB stadiums this year was John Fogerty's "Centerfield."

What baseball fan doesn't love that song? It's catchy and beautifully captures the charm of the national pastime. "Centerfield's" opening handclaps are as iconic as peanuts, popcorn, and crackerjacks.

Fogerty released two solo albums after leaving Creedence Clearwater Revival. Neither of which faired particularly well. A legal battle with his record label led to his refusing to record for the next decade.

When he finally returned to the music scene, "Centerfield" was Fogerty's first release. He wrote the lyrics, played all the instruments, and produced the track, which now plays on continuous loop at the Baseball Hall of Fame in Cooperstown, New York.

"When I was a little kid, there were no teams on the West Coast," Fogerty told *MLB.com*. "I'd hear about (Babe) Ruth and (Joe) DiMaggio, and as my dad and older brothers talked about the Babe's exploits, their eyes would get so big."

Fogerty grew to think of center field at Yankee Stadium as being "the most hallowed place in all of the universe."

Most people interpret the song as being a cry for playing time. They envision an eager player begging his coach for a chance at glory. *Put me in coach, I'm ready to play today.*

But there's another contingency who chose to interpret the song as being more symbolic of a humble player affirming his willingness to embrace whatever is asked him. *Put me in coach, I'm ready to play today—and I'm willing to do whatever you need me to do.*

The first player has an entitled mindset. He wants to play because he believes he's better than the players who are playing. He wants an opportunity to prove his belief.

The second player has a servant's mindset. He loves his team and is excited for an opportunity to contribute in any way he can.

Put me in coach, I can be center field.

At higher levels, the center fielder is revered. It's an important position. Some of the game's greatest players—DiMaggio, Willie Mays, Mickey Mantle, and Ty Cobb—played center field. As Fogerty told *The New York Times*, the center fielder is "the king, the head of the tribe, the most special one."

That's not usually the case at lower levels. Center field is far less heralded in little league. Coaches usually hide the weakest players in the outfield. The position is not seen as a glamorous assignment.

This distinction plays into the song's interpretation. The first player wants the attention and accolades that come with playing center field—for himself. The second player is willing to accept the lack of esteem that comes with playing center field—for his team.

The second player's motives are in keeping with an individual who aspires to be a good teammate. Putting someone with his attitude into the lineup can change the game's flow for the better. His is an attitude worthy of being "waved home."

As always…Good teammates care. Good teammates share. Good teammates listen. Go be a good teammate.

*The MLB.com *quote referenced above is from Singer, Tom. "Put Him in, Coach: Fogerty to Play at Hall." May 25, 2010. http://mlb.mlb.com/news/article_entertainment.jsp?ymd=20100524&content_id=10399462&vkey=entertainment&fext=.jsp*

**John Fogerty's *New York Times *quote referenced above is from Kepner, Tyler. "John Fogerty Tells the Story Behind 'Centerfield'." May 24, 2010. https://archive.nytimes.com/bats.blogs.nytimes.com/2010/05/24/john-fogerty-tells-the-story-behind-centerfield/*

Your Best Service
NOVEMBER 15

I try to steer *Teammate Tuesdays* clear of negativity. But over the course of the last month, I've witnessed three customer service failures—all defended by the pretense of the business being *short-staffed*—that merit discussion.

The first occurred at an ice cream stand. I had stopped to reward my daughters with a treat. The line to order at the walk-up window wasn't especially long, but it curiously seemed to be moving unusually slow. As I got closer to the window, I noticed there were only two employees inside, neither of which seemed thrilled to be working.

While we were waiting, one of the employees ripped the window open and yelled, "We're short staffed, so you're all just going to have to be patient."

When a customer in front of me tried to explain that what she had been given was not what she ordered, the same employee told her, "Well, we're short-staffed. So that's what you got." The employee then proceeded to slam the window shut without attempting to correct the mistake.

The second incident happened at a bank. I've been doing business with this bank for years, but this was the first time I had ever used this particular branch location. When I entered, an employee leaning against the outside of the lobby counter, who later identified himself as the branch manager, asked if he could help me.

I told him I wanted to make a deposit. To my surprise, he replied that they couldn't take any deposits. He said they were short-staffed and that both of his tellers were out sick. When I asked why he, the branch manager, couldn't process the transaction, he implied the task was beneath him by snarking: "I can't do that."

The third incident happened at a coffee shop. They were open but had shut off their mobile ordering and locked their lobby doors. A long drive-thru line wrapped around their building and a group of angry customers gathered near the shop's entrance.

After multiple customers tried to unsuccessfully enter, an annoyed employee came to door and told the crowd they were "short-staffed" and only taking drive-thru orders. Her discourteousness further inflamed the crowd.

I counted at least six baristas "working" inside the shop, although I'm not certain that word applied to all of them as some were standing around, casually talking to one another.

Each of these incidents involved unsatisfactory customer service. And each of them violated a key good teammate principle: *Having a bad day doesn't excuse you to be a bad teammate.*

Being "short staffed" can be taxing. The situation can cause operations to be less efficient and team members to bear a heavier burden. To those who are present, it's often unfair and unpleasant.

But the unpleasantness of the situation doesn't have to be projected onto the customer.

Take the coffee shop incident described above. The staff was rude, inconsiderate, unapologetic, and chose a convenient solution. Because they were doing business under less-than-ideal circumstances, they acted as though they were entitled to their customers' empathy.

Their response created angry, frustrated customers. I left that coffee shop and walked to the next closest location. Same franchise. Same number of staff working inside. Same long drive-thru line wrapping around the building. Only this location had its lobby open and was taking mobile orders.

The second location's staff was managing the difficult situation much differently. They were welcoming, hustling, working together, and utilizing creativity to solve the problem—even though doing so was inconvenient for them.

They were handling the situation with *good teammate moves* and a good teammate mindset. Their response created appreciative, understanding customers.

When you're part of a team, you serve the needs of your team. This applies to sports teams, sales teams, leadership teams, and anyone in the service industry.

You won't always feel good, be in a good mood, or operate under optimal conditions. However, none of those reasons should ever diminish your commitment to being a good teammate to those you serve.

Providing quality service doesn't require you to subscribe to the belief that the customer is always right, but it does require you to accept the premise that the customer *always* deserves your best service.

As always...Good teammates care. Good teammates share. Good teammates listen. Go be a good teammate.

The Balloon Handlers
NOVEMBER 22

Having an "attitude of gratitude" is crucial to being a good teammate. In the past, my Thanksgiving week topics have focused on the value of gratitude.

This year, I'd like to highlight an often unnoticed entity associated with Thanksgiving who embodies another important *good teammate* skill—the ability to adjust.

My family's Thanksgiving Day routine consists of us getting up, eating a light breakfast, watching the Macy's Parade while we prepare our Thanksgiving meal, feasting, watching football, napping (usually while watching football), and feasting again.

I enjoy each of those activities, but I am most partial to watching the Macy's Thanksgiving Day Parade. My favorite part of the parade is the giant balloons.

Giant balloons have been a parade staple since 1927. The balloons replaced the Central Park Zoo animals that appeared in the inaugural parade, three years earlier.

Felix the Cat was the first balloon to appear in the parade. Snoopy has appeared in the most parades (40) and Ronald McDonald has the current streak for most consecutive appearances (28).

The helium-filled balloons are about five stories high and 60 feet long. Each balloon requires around 90 handlers. Depending on the year, there are between 2,000 to 3,000 balloon handlers walking in the parade.

Being a balloon handler is harder than most think. In a 2021 *USA Today* article, adventure journalist Kate McCarthy described the experience as follows:

"Imagine holding a resistance band at its tautest, your biceps strain and your core is fully engaged, that is what it feels like to hold one of those giant balloons. Throw in a few gusts of wind, and you can see why it takes so many people to handle these absolute beasts."

The job of a parade balloon handler is a continuous battle to adjust. They must adjust the pace at which they walk. They must adjust the amount of slack they give their rope. They must adjust the grip on their "bones"—the proper term for the balloon's handles.

And they must make all those adjustments in concert with their fellow balloon handlers.

Failing to make necessary adjustments could cause the balloon's lines to get tangled, the balloon to turn in the wrong direction, or something much worse.

Being a good teammate is a similar battle of continuous adjustment. You must adjust to your competition. You must adjust to the elements. You must adjust to your teams' circumstances if someone gets injured, falls ill, or otherwise becomes unavailable.

And, like a balloon handler, you must make all those adjustments in concert with your fellow teammates.

Failing to make adjustments could cause your team to become entangled in drama, head in the wrong direction, or something much worse.

The best balloon handlers and the best teammates are not only willing to make adjustments, they are grateful for the opportunity to do so. That's why both smile while doing their jobs.

As always…Good teammates care. Good teammates share. Good teammates listen. Go be a good teammate.

Kate McCarthy's USA Today quote from above can be found at McCarthy, Kate. "Join in on the fun: What's it like to hold up a balloon in Macy's Thanksgiving Day Parade?" November 26, 2021. https://www.usatoday.com/story/life/2021/11/26/whats-like-hold-up-balloon-macys-thanksgiving-day-parade/8753139002/

Undervalued Fountains
NOVEMBER 29

The fastest growing form of housing in the United States today are *common-interest-developments*—properties governed by a homeowners association (HOA).

HOA board members are charged with enforcing community standards and implementing bylaws that serve the greater needs of the community. Maintaining a civil decorum can be challenging when community and individual interests fail to align.

Anyone who has ever served on an HOA board knows it is a thankless job, fraught with pettiness and stress.

Recently, a member of an HOA board was telling me about a controversy brewing in their community. The wiring to a large in-pond fountain near their development's entrance had deteriorated and needed to be replaced.

Bids to repair the fountain came in considerably higher than expected and now many residents are lobbying to forgo the repairs in favor of eliminating the fountain. They feel that paying that much for what is tantamount to "eye candy" is wasting the community's money. However, the HOA board viewed making the repairs as the best use of the community's money. In their opinion, fountains are more than just "eye candy." Fountains provide aeration, reduce algae growth, eliminate odors, decrease insects, and give fish and other pond inhabitants a healthy habitat.

The HOA board believed the long-term financial benefits of repairing the fountain vastly outweigh the short-term savings of eliminating it.

Good teammates are a lot like fountains. They discharge positivity, which returns to the team and gets recirculated amongst the members. Good teammates also reduce toxicity, decrease drama, and facilitate a healthy team environment.

And, like fountains, the extent of their contributions tend to be overlooked and undervalued.

When it comes to team culture, the long-term benefits of having kind, caring, considerate *good* teammates vastly outweigh the short-term benefits of having talented, self-centered individuals on the team. The former will see the team through tough times. The latter will inevitably cause tough times—and abandon the team as soon as that happens.

If you've got a good teammate on your team who is struggling with their performance, consider investing in their "repair" before you elect to eliminate them. Doing so may turn out to be the most rewarding investment you will ever make.

As always…Good teammates care. Good teammates share. Good teammates listen. Go be a good teammate.

Swift Thinking
DECEMBER 6

The holiday season always causes an interesting disruption to the music charts. This week, four of the top ten songs on the *Billboard Hot 100* are Christmas classics—Mariah Carey's "All I Want for Christmas" (5), Brenda Lee's "Rockin' Around the Christmas Tree" (6), Bobby Helms' "Jingle Bell Rock" (9), and Burl Ives' "A Holly Jolly Christmas" (10).

Those Christmas classics have upended the standing of many contemporary hits, but not all of them. For the fifth week in a row, the chart's top spot belongs to Taylor Swift's catchy anthem about insecurity and anxiety, "Anti-Hero."

"Anti-Hero" is Swift's ninth number-one single, making her the only solo artist in *Billboard* history to debut five songs atop the charts. You don't have to be a *Swiftie* (a devout fan of all things Taylor Swift) to appreciate the song's lyrical genius.

Nor do you have to be a "good teammate" expert to appreciate the relevance several of those clever lyrics have to the art of being a good teammate. For example:

I should not be left to my own devices, they come with prices and vices, I end up in crisis

Vices do indeed come with prices. And when you're part of a team, the price of your bad habits is usually your team's well-being. We are ultimately defined by our habits. Vices—bad, disruptive, inconsiderate, selfish habits—prevent teams from reaching a level of productivity conducive to achievement. If left unchecked, vices will spiral a team into crisis. Good teammates avert team crises by eliminating their personal vices.

Did you hear my covert narcissism I disguise as altruism...

Narcissists—individuals stuck in the *ME* gear—have an unreasonably high sense of their own importance. They seek attention and want people to admire them. When narcissists make good teammate moves, they tend to turn around and say, "Hey, did you see what I just did? Wasn't that kind of me? Aren't you in awe of my generosity?" Good teammates don't operate that way. Their altruistic behavior is always sincere. They never have hidden agendas or ulterior motives. To good teammates, altruism is such a part of their identity that it makes actions like turning away from someone in need unimaginable.

I'll stare directly at the sun but never in the mirror

Isn't it odd that some of the seemingly toughest people are paradoxically not strong enough to engage in self-assessment? They're able to fearlessly confront dangers that immobilize others, yet they're unable to face their own demons. Good teammates possess the courage and humility to self-assess because they're driven to be their best—*for their teams*. Their willingness to *stare in the mirror* affords them a sense of inner peace.

A final "Anti-Hero" lyrical thought: Rooting for an anti-hero is exhausting, but rooting for a good teammate is exhilarating. Their presence is never the problem; it's always the solution.

As always…Good teammates care. Good teammates share. Good teammates listen. Go be a good teammate.

The Five Teammates Everybody Needs
DECEMBER 13

When NASA encounters a problem, they don't task one engineer to resolve it. They assign the problem to a *team* of engineers. Google, Apple, Meta and nearly every other industry leader take the same approach.

The most daunting problems are always best handled by a team effort—including bullying.

Recently, I was asked to speak to a group of parents and educators about how the art of being a good teammate relates to bullying. Good teammates don't bully, nor do they tend to be bullied.

If someone you know is being bullied, one of the best approaches you can take is to encourage them to become a "good teammate." Relatedly, you should try to help them assemble a team to tackle their problem.

Here are five teammates everyone needs—especially those being bullied:

1. **Upstander**

   An Upstander is someone who refuses to be a bystander. They won't stand idly by and watch others be bullied. They stand up for the bullied through their words and their actions. Upstanders have moxie, and they aren't afraid to use it.

   Where do you find them? Upstanders are usually peers, siblings, or older acquaintances. Sadly, you don't find them; they find you. But you can get on their radar by being kind, offering compliments, and conveying gratitude. People tend to defend those who make them feel good about themselves.

2. **Mentor**

   A Mentor is someone whose example you want to emulate. They model enviable behaviors and guide you through the uncertainty of how to appropriately respond to difficult situations.

   Where do you find them? Mentors are typically teachers, coaches, older siblings, or experienced associates. In dysfunctional environments, where none of the aforementioned are available, you may need to turn to books, television, or movies. Fictional characters can be effective mentors under the right circumstances.

3. **Champion**

As the name suggests, a Champion is someone who will *champion* your cause. They're invested in your problems to the point that *your* problems become *their* problems. Champions are essential to those struggling with learning disabilities, body image issues, or any attribute that makes them a target for bullying.

Where do you find them? Champions are typically teachers, coaches, counselors, therapists, or parents. (*I would argue that it's every parent's job to be a Champion for their child!) You find them in schools, extracurricular activities, help centers, and, of course, loving homes.

4. **Buddy**

A buddy is someone who can commiserate with your problems because they're facing the same challenges. They understand the hurt you're feeling.

Where do you find them? Buddies must be peers or near peers, otherwise it will be hard for them to truly relate to what you're experiencing. You find Buddies in extracurricular activities, clubs, and support groups. Ironically, you probably won't find them by sitting on a Buddy Bench. Unless someone's already sitting there, plopping down on a Buddy Bench might yield you a Champion or Upstander—but not likely a Buddy.

5. Resonator

A resonator is someone who emits good vibes. Their positivity is contagious and inspires you to want to be a better version of yourself. They possess a cheerful disposition capable of improving your worst mood.

Where do you find them? Resonators are everywhere! Just look for enthusiastic personalities who are perpetually happy, and you'll find them. By the way, Resonators don't have to be humans. Pets can be excellent Resonators.

According to a study by the National Center on Addiction and Substance Abuse (N.C.A.S.A.) at Columbia University, 64% of bullied middle schoolers will use drugs before they graduate high school. Tragedies like those in Uvalde, Oxford, and Parkland demonstrate that drug use isn't the worse bullying outcome. Helping someone who's being bullied procure these five teammates could be a contribution of life-altering significance.

As always…Good teammates care. Good teammates share. Good teammates listen. Go be a good teammate.

The NCASA study referenced above can be found at www.addictionguide.com/addiction/bullying/

Learning From Christmas Villains
DECEMBER 20

Are you a fan of Christmas movies? How about Christmas movie villains? As the expression goes, we learn from everyone we encounter. Sometimes it's what to do; sometimes it's what not to do.

In that spirit, here are ten bad attributes that keep these Christmas movie antagonists from being good teammates:

10. Ebenezer Scrooge
A Christmas Carol (2009)

Ebenezer Scrooge has many faults, but his most notable is greed. He is the quintessential cold-hearted miser. He values money more than anyone or anything. Good teammates are not greedy. They're altruistic and appreciate their teams' human capital.

9. Scut Farkus

A Christmas Story (1983)

Scut Farkus is mean, nasty, and shallow. He is a bully who relishes opportunities to terrorize Ralphie and the rest of his "nameless rabble of victims." Good teammates don't bully. They stand up for the bullied.

8. Harry & Marv, The Wet Bandits

Home Alone (1990)

In addition to their thievery, The Wet Bandits are deceitful. They routinely pass themselves off as being something they are not. Good teammates are not phony. They are always genuine, as are their intentions.

7. Jack Frost

The Santa Claus 3: The Escape Clause (2006)

Jack Frost is the figure responsible for snow, ice, and unpleasantly cold weather. (Villainous enough in many circles!) This dreadful schemer is cunning and manipulative—and envious. Santa gets "Coca-Cola cans and TV specials," while he's stuck with a "few runny noses and some dead citrus." Good teammates don't envy other team members. They are happy for their teammates' good fortune.

6. Mr. Potter

It's a Wonderful Life (1946)

Cut from the same fabric as Scrooge, Mr. Potter is the robber baron who sends George Bailey's life into peril. Mr. Potter is unempathetic to the hurting residents of Bedford Falls. Good teammates don't have hardened hearts. They are compassionate and aware of the impact their actions have on others.

5. Hans Gruber

Die Hard (1988)

Whether or not *Die Hard* is a Christmas movie may be subject to discussion, but the fact that Hans Gruber is a violent terrorist is not. Hans Gruber is downright ruthless. Good teammates are not cruel nor merciless. And they don't hold others emotionally hostage. They treat everyone with kindness and respect.

4. Oogie Boogie

A Nightmare Before Christmas (1993)

Oogie Boogie, Jack Skellington's vile nemesis, is "the embodiment of a child's worst nightmare." He's heinous, boisterous, and uses fear to intimidate others. Good teammates don't lead with fear. They have the confidence to lead with love.

3. The Grinch

Dr. Seuss' How the Grinch Stole Christmas (1966)

The Grinch is as cuddly as a cactus and as charming as an eel. This cantankerous recluse is indeed a "mean one." Good teammates are not cranky. They are perpetually cheerful and well-aware of the contagiousness of their emotions.

2. Mayor Augustus Maywho

How the Grinch Stole Christmas (2000)

The Grinch isn't the only Dr. Seuss character to make the list. Whoville's vain, arrogant mayor, August Maywho, bullied the Grinch as a child and is responsible for the Grinch's hatred of Christmas. The word that best describes Mayor Maywho is self-serving. His own interests are his sole concern. Good teammates are not self-serving. They put their teams' interests ahead of their own.

1. Frank Shirley

National Lampoon's Christmas Vacation (1989)

Could anything be worse than a boss who gifts his employees a membership to the "Jelly of the Month Club" as a Christmas bonus? Contrary to Cousin Eddie's assertion, that isn't a "gift that keeps on giving the whole year." Frank Shirley is cheap, pompous, and inconsiderate. Good teammates are none of those. They are generous, humble, and highly considerate.

Fortunately, nearly everyone on this list demonstrates themselves capable of redemption. If you happen to suffer from any of the above shortcomings, know that you too are redeemable.

As always…Good teammates care. Good teammates share. Good teammates listen. Go be a good teammate—and have a Merry Christmas!

The Year in Review
DECEMBER 27

We strive to share the sort of meaningful social media content that inspires readers to want to be better teammates. The fruits of our labor have continued to bless us with a loyal online following.

In keeping with our annual year-end tradition, here are the posts from each of the past twelve months that received the most interactions, impressions, shares, likes, retweets, and favorites across all our social media channels:

JANUARY

"You can leave a legacy by being a good teammate. People will forget the scores, records, and statistics...but they will never forget how a fellow teammate made them feel."

FEBRUARY

"Good teammates get ahead by not letting others fall behind. WE>me."

MARCH

"Good teammates stand up for those who cannot stand up for themselves. Watching someone be cruel and doing nothing about it is the same as being cruel. #courage."

APRIL

"Those who don't believe in heroes have never had a good teammate. (One good teammate can change everything!)"

MAY

"A willingness to listen demonstrates a willingness to learn. #theWEgear"

JUNE

"Good teammates are the magical ingredient in every successful team. Teamwork doesn't happen without good teammates."

JULY

"Unshared knowledge is just another form of selfishness. (Good teammates unselfishly share what they know with their fellow teammates—because doing so helps their TEAM.) #theWEgear #mindset."

AUGUST

"Silence equates to approval. When toxicity threatens your team, speak up."

SEPTEMBER

"If you have the patience to endure, you have the ability to conquer. Sometimes success comes from hanging on after others have left go."

OCTOBER

"Good teammates are defined by the consistency of their commitment. It's not what you occasionally do; it's what you CONSISTENTLY do."

NOVEMBER

"Having a bad day does not excuse you to be a bad teammate. Just because things aren't going your way doesn't mean you get to speak rudely, act selfishly, or behave badly toward others. Good teammates become the mood their team needs from them. WE before me. #BeAGoodTeammate

DECEMBER

"The size of your ego should not surpass the size of your heart. When you're part of a team, humility and kindness matter."

Please continue to support our Good Teammate efforts, as we strive to reach a larger audience and inspire even more individuals to become better teammates.

If you know of someone who could benefit from a dose of the Good Teammate message, please encourage them to join the conversation and start following us on social media. They can connect with us on the following sites:

Facebook: *https://www.facebook.com/coachloya*
Twitter: *https://twitter.com/coachlanceloya*
Instagram: *https://www.instagram.com/lanceloya*
LinkedIn: *https://www.linkedin.com/in/coachloya*

As always…Good teammates care. Good teammates share. Good teammates listen. Go be a good teammate.

The S.E.A. Approach
JANUARY 3

The novelty of a clean slate eases the challenge of altering our habits. Hence, the start of a new year is viewed by many as the opportune time to adopt a resolution, set a goal, or embrace a life theme. Plenty start the New Year fueled with ambition. But then life happens. They get distracted. Then, they get discouraged. And before they know it, their ambition turns into abandonment.

I used to be someone who suffered through this cycle.

My biggest obstacle was that I usually chose conflicting resolutions and/or goals. I aspired to exercise more, travel more, sleep more, spend more time with my family, and learn more skills.

Despite my best efforts, I continually found myself unable to reengineer the mathematical confines of a twenty-four-hour day. I simply couldn't fit all those resolutions and goals into my life without eliminating something I was currently doing—a premise that contributed to me abandoning my New Year's ambitions.

After a conversation I had with an older, wiser mentor, I decided to take a S.E.A. approach to the turning of the calendar. Each year, I pick two areas of my life to sustain, two to expand, and two to amend.

SUSTAIN

My receptiveness to change has led me to develop several "good" habits that I don't want to abandon. In fact, quite the opposite, I want to make a conscious effort to sustain these habits.

For instance, my wife, who is also my business partner, and I go on a thirty minute walk every morning where we discuss pressing business matters. We think of these walks as a moving staff meeting. They've proven to be beneficial on multiple fronts and, therefore, I am committed to keeping them going. I may have to compromise a few of my other practices to make room for new ambitions, but I refuse to allow our staff meeting walks to be discarded or altered.

EXPAND

I don't want to be the same version of myself next year as I currently am—in *every* regard. So I aspire to expand my sphere of experiences, which expands my comfort zone and the extent of my knowledge.

I have been to all but five of the Hard Rock Cafés in the United States. This year, my goal is to visit and buy a t-shirt from at least one of my remaining locations (Sacramento, Memphis, Honolulu, Denver, and Cincinnati).

This isn't so much a resolution as it is a goal, albeit a silly one to some. But it's my goal and its worthiness is relative to me. Having something to look forward to, to pursue, keeps life interesting.

AMEND

Just as I have habits I want to keep, I also have habits I want to amend. I don't know that they need to be completely abandoned, but they do need to be altered for the better.

I've been drinking too much coffee lately. A little coffee has arguable health benefits; a lot of coffee has none. I've decided that I am going to limit my coffee intake to only those occasions when I am writing. I don't write every day, nor do I write more than once a day. So linking my coffee intake to my writing habits seems like a pairing that will bear dividends.

The objective of New Year's resolutions, goals, and themes should be to make you a better version of yourself, whether that means being happier, healthier, or holier.

Notable seafarer Jacques Cousteau once said, a changed life happens when you "discard the old, embrace the new, and run headlong down an immutable course." The S.E.A. approach will assuredly lead you in that direction.

As always…Good teammates care. Good teammates share. Good teammates listen. Go be a good teammate.

Turning Toward Connectivity
JANUARY 10

January is the busiest month of the year for online dating. Apps like Tinder, Bumble, and OkCupid all experience a surge in signups and activity this month.

Based on last year's data, January activity on OkCupid alone will lead to more than 40 million new matches.

The timing of the dating app surge makes sense much in the same way that the increase in January gym memberships makes sense: *New Year, new you.* The hustle and bustle of the holidays is over. It's time to upgrade your love life. And, of course, the Valentine's Day clock is ticking.

So what are dating app users most looking for in their new relationships?

It's hard to pinpoint. A Google search for "what people are most looking for in a relationship" produces more than three billion results. Among those on the first page are several credible articles who claim trust, honesty, kindness, and the ability to be yourself to be the top answers.

While there may be no clear consensus on what people are most looking for in relationships, psychologists John and Julie Gottman believe they have identified the "number one thing" that makes relationships successful—how a couple responds to *bids for connection.*

The Gottman's, founders of the Gottman Institute and the world famous "Love Lab," have been studying romantic relationships for more than fifty years. Malcolm Gladwell featured their work in his *New York Times* bestseller, *Blink.*

In the Gottman's most recent study, they determined the biggest factor in predicting a marriage's longevity was how often a couple "turned toward" their partner.

"When a couple turns toward each other, they make and respond to what we call 'bids for connection.' Bids can range from little things, like trying to catch your attention by calling your name, to big things, like asking for deeper needs to be met,' the Gottman's told CNBC.com.

Let's say your partner is looking at their phone and says, "Oh, this is interesting." How do you respond?

Do you turn *toward* them? (i.e., acknowledge their attempt to connect, inquire about what they saw, join the moment, etc.)

Do you turn *away* from them? (i.e., not notice their attempt to connect, actively ignore them, continue with what you're doing, etc.)

Or, do you turn *against* them? (i.e. shut down their attempt to connect, become angry or irritated, scold them for interrupting your work, etc.)

According to the Gottmans, the happiest couples recognize when counterparts are making bids and stop what they're doing to engage. In other words, they turn toward each other.

Successful relationships, whether they're between couples or teammates, rely on connectivity. Both parties must strive to create, maintain, and validate sound connections.

The next time you feel inclined to assess your relationships with your teammates, think about how you respond to their bids to connect. Do you turn toward, away, or against? Your answer may be the key to improving your team's connectedness.

And if you happen to be among the millions utilizing an online dating app this month, take time to evaluate your match's response to your bids to connect. Swipe right on the ones who turn toward you. They're demonstrating a capacity to be a good teammate.

As always…Good teammates care. Good teammates share. Good teammates listen. Go be a good teammate.

*The OKCupid data referenced above can be found at https://theblog.okcupid.com/the-global-state-of-digital-dating-2eac672fcb3e

**The Gottman study referenced above is from Buehlman, K. T., Gottman, J. M., and Katz, L. F. (1992). "How a couple views their past predicts their future: Predicting divorce from an oral history interview." Journal of Family Psychology, 5(3-4), 295–318. https://doi.org/10.1037/0893-3200.5.3-4.295

***The Gottman's CNBC.com quote referenced above is from "Here's the No. 1 thing that makes relationships successful, say psychologists who studied 40,000 couples." November 11, 2022. https://www.cnbc.com/2022/11/11/the-no-relationship-hack-according-to-psychologists-who-have-been-married-for-35-years.html

Redemption Through Reinvention
JANUARY 17

How you handle making a mistake says a lot about your ability to be a good teammate. Your willingness to admit your mistake, own it, atone for it, and commit to not repeating it are important steps to putting the mistake behind you.

In most cases, these steps will restore you to a place of good standing on your team. But what about when they don't? What happens when your attempts to atone fail to bring you redemption? This situation can be frustrating—for you and your teammates. You want everything to go back to how it was before your transgression. You resent now being subjected to your teammates' skepticism and added scrutiny.

Your teammates resent that you *resent* being subjected to skepticism and added scrutiny. They're bothered by what they perceive to be your unmerited entitlement to a clean slate.

Continuing this resentful exchange will only widen the divide between you and your teammates. If you want to heal your team, you must first understand that forgiveness does not equate to redemption. Furthermore, you must understand that your mistake transformed who you are in your teammates' eyes. You messed up. You hurt your team by selfishly choosing to do something you knew to be wrong. No amount of apologizing or penance will change those facts. You are now a different person.

There's an analogy used in addiction recovery that applies here: *You were once a cucumber, but now you're a pickle, and you can never turn a pickle back into a cucumber.*

Once you accept this premise, you begin to focus on creating the future and abandon trying to fix the past. Whatever mistake you made altered how your teammates view you. Rather than pouring your energy into trying to change their perspective, use the circumstances as a catalyst to reinvent yourself.

Take the steps to admit, own, apologize, and atone for your mistake. Commit to not repeating it. Embrace your teammates' skepticism and added scrutiny without discontent. Then, free yourself from the confines of resent.

Become an unentitled version of yourself who relishes the opportunity to serve the needs of your team, regardless of what others think. Let your new attitude become your defining characteristic.

You aren't a cucumber anymore. You're a pickle. And pickles are revered for being good pickles, not for the cucumbers they used to be.

As always…Good teammates care. Good teammates share. Good teammates listen. Go be a good teammate.

How Compliments Complement
JANUARY 24

Today is National Compliment Day! Created in the late 1990s by Debby Hoffman and Kathy Chamberlin, authors of the book *Find Something Nice to Say*, the date reminds us to use our words to brighten someone else's day.

Compliments make people feel good, build trust, and increase the likelihood of positive behaviors being repeated— all outcomes that contribute to a winning team culture.

Hence, good teammates are never stingy with sincere compliments. They give them consistently and abundantly because they know compliments *complement*.

In grammatical terms, compliment and complement are homophones, words that sound the same but have different meanings or spellings.

A compliment is an expression of praise or admiration. It's telling someone "Good job." It's letting them know their courage is inspiring or their fashion sense is amazing.

A complement is something that improves another or brings it to perfection, like adding a pocket square to an elegant suit or a belt to a stylish dress. The right lipstick can complement the color of a woman's eyes. The right wine can complement the taste of a steak.

Both words are rooted in the Latin word *complēre* which means "to complete."

When you give a teammate a compliment you endear yourself to the recipient. Your kindness imprints on their soul and their response imprints on yours. The exchange increases your connectivity, thereby increasing the team's connectivity.

A connected team experiences better communication, higher investment, and a greater chance of completing its mission.

Research shows those short interactions where you tell someone they did a good job and they subsequently thank you for recognizing their efforts have a bigger impact on relationships than most realize. The recipient experiences increased activity in the area of the brain associated with rewards, and so does the giver.

Think of the iconic line from the movie *Jerry Maguire* where Tom Cruise tells Rene Zellweger: "You complete me." The line brought tears to both of their eyes. His words were a compliment. Speaking them led to a connection that complemented their lives.

The same happens to teams whose teammates pay compliments to each other.

Today, make a point to compliment your teammates. Let someone know they're doing nice work. Tell someone you're moved by their passion. Convey to someone how much their smile brightens your day. Then do the same tomorrow. And the day after that, too. Doing so will validate their actions and bring value to your team.

As always...Good teammates care. Good teammates share. Good teammates listen. Go be a good teammate.

The interaction research referenced above is from Boothby, E. J., and Bohns, V. K. (2021). "Why a Simple Act of Kindness Is Not as Simple as It Seems: Underestimating the Positive Impact of Our Compliments on Others." Personality and Social Psychology Bulletin, 47(5), 826–840. https://doi.org/10.1177/0146167220949003

Sandpaper Teammates
JANUARY 31

Woodworking is a trade that requires creativity, dexterity, and patience—a lot of patience. To produce a quality product, no part of the carpentry process should be rushed. Diligence matters at every stage, especially when it comes to sanding.

I've yet to come across a woodworker who discounts the value of sanding. Not only does sanding produce a smooth, appealing finish, it prevents splintering, removes milling imperfections, and improves finish adhesion.

Saws and planers tend to crush the wood's fibers and clog the pores, which prevent stains and varnishes from being absorbed. Sanding reopens those pores, thereby strengthening the finish's bond.

Like woodworking, teambuilding requires patience—a lot of patience. That is, patience with everything *except* toxic behaviors.

To ensure a healthy team environment, culturally disruptive behaviors must be confronted with expedition. A slow response allows toxicity to gain a foothold.

Unfortunately, confrontation is often followed by contempt. People don't like having their egos *roughed* up. An unpleasant confrontation can leave both parties feeling angry, hurt, and bitter.

Though understandable, none of those reactions provide the ideal foundation for improving a team's cohesiveness.

That's why teams benefit from having *sandpaper teammates*—individuals capable of smoothing over the disdain caused by confrontation and internal conflict.

Sandpaper teammates are master empathizers. They appreciate the hurt caused by the confrontation, as well as the need for the confrontation. This skill positions them to replace emotional subjectivity with rational objectivity.

Having someone on the team who can convey understanding with a calming tone reduces the risk of necessary confrontations turning into unnecessary feuds.

Sandpaper comes in a variety of coarseness, measured in grit. Paper with larger granules have a lower grit rating. Paper with smaller granules have a higher grit rating. When sanding wood, the higher the grit, the finer the finish.

This rating system applies to sandpaper teammates too. In the context of behavior, grit is a personality trait demonstrated through passion and perseverance toward a goal despite being challenged by obstacles.

New York Times bestselling author and pioneering psychologist Angela Duckwoth says grit is the "hallmark of high achievers in every domain."

The grittier sandpaper teammates are, the more effective they are in their role. Their grittiness prevents the team from splintering, removes imperfections, and strengthens their teams' bonds—all of which contribute to a quality team finish.

As always…Good teammates care. Good teammates share. Good teammates listen. Go be a good teammate.

Freed From Mental Slavery
FEBRUARY 7

Three weeks ago, I wrote a blog about the way good teammates handle mistakes titled "Redemption Through Reinvention."

I heard from a number of readers afterwards how timely what I wrote was for them and their teams, as they were being challenged by the issues I described. Interestingly, several of the messages I received referenced Bob Marley's "Redemption Song."

I love that song.

Regarded by many as *the* anthem of emancipation, "Redemption Song" was written during a tenuous time in Marley's life. The reggae legend had been diagnosed with cancer several months prior and was aware that his time on Earth was nearing its end.

Marley recorded fifteen different variations of the song, but an unaccompanied acoustic version played in the key of G major seemed to best capture his emotional state at the time. That solo acoustic recording became the final track of *Uprising*—the last Bob Marley & the Wailers album released during the singer's lifetime.

Of the many beautiful lines in "Redemption Song," the one that should resonate the most with aspiring good teammates is:

> *Emancipate yourself from mental slavery, None but ourselves can free our minds.*

That line was inspired by a passage in a speech Marcus Garvey, a Jamaican political activist, entrepreneur, Pan-African civil rights leader, and one of Marley's heroes, delivered to a Nova Scotian audience in 1937:

> *"We are going to emancipate ourselves from mental slavery because whilst others might free the body, none but ourselves can free the mind. Mind is your only ruler, sovereign. The man who is not able to develop and use his mind is bound to be the slave of the other man who uses his mind."*

Many times, it is the mental stranglehold people have on themselves that keeps them from being good teammates.

They allow regret, resentment, and insecurity to constrain their productivity. They allow frustration with circumstances beyond their control to confine their adaptivity. And they allow indifference to cloud their objectivity.

By failing to *emancipate* their negative thoughts, they restrict their capacity to effectively serve the needs of their teams and put themselves at risk of being a source of team toxicity.

As both Marley and Garvey allude, good teammates know they're the ones responsible for freeing their minds from mindsets that are detrimental to their teams.

Marley died in May 1981, less than a year after "Redemption Song" was released. He would have celebrated his seventy-eighth birthday this week.

To honor his memory, share the brilliance of his message this week with someone who needs a dose of hope. Doing so might very well be the enlightenment that helps them free their mind from mental slavery.

As always…Good teammates care. Good teammates share. Good teammates listen. Go be a good teammate.

Matters of Your Time
FEBRUARY 14

Happy Valentines Day! Is it just me or does the arrival of this holiday seem anticlimactic? Almost every store I've entered since the day after Christmas has been inundated with red hearts.

The heart has a curious connection to love. No one really knows how or why the heart came to be the symbol of love. Although there seems to be plenty of theories explaining the relationship.

Some link the connection to strong emotions, like love, causing our hearts to beat noticeably faster during romantic encounters.

Some trace it to the shape of the leaves of a silphium plant, a now extinct species of fennel that ancient civilizations used for its contraceptive properties in love potions.

Others believe the connection stems from the legend of Venus, the goddess of love, setting hearts on fire while her son, Cupid, shot arrows into his targets' hearts, thereby causing them uncontrollable attraction.

Still, others credit the connection to the martyred priest, Saint Valentine, who supposedly used the symbol of the heart as a code when arranging secret marriages.

Dr. Marilyn Yalom, former Stanford professor and author of the book *The Amorous Heart: An Unconventional History of Love*, devoted an entire TEDx talk to exploring the symbology of the heart and debunking some of the above myths.

Personally, I think the image of an hourglass would be a more appropriate symbol of love than the heart.

For starters, love and other related emotions are actually regulated in the part of the brain called the hypothalamus, not the heart.

I doubt the image of the brain would make a better symbol for love, however. Anyone who has dabbled in love will attest that decisions related to love are rarely made with your head.

Love, romantic or otherwise, isn't really a matter of your heart nor your head. Love is a matter of your time. When you love someone, or something, you gift that entity your time— your most valuable possession.

You *choose* to invest your time in what you love. Time is perishable. It cannot be renewed nor banked. Once it's gone; it's gone. Hence, devoting time to *anything* is an outward sign of what is important to you.

This is certainly true when it comes to good teammates and the love they have for their teams.

Sacrificing their time listening to a teammate vent, encouraging a distraught teammate, or assisting an overburdened teammate conveys their love for their team.

For good teammates, caring is sharing their time with their teammates.

Don't waste the sands in your hourglass. Be sure to express your love for your team today with the gift of your time. I promise it's a gift that matters.

As always…Good teammates care. Good teammates share. Good teammates listen. Go be a good teammate.

Dr. Marilyn Yalom's TEDx talk referenced above can be viewed at https://www.youtube.com/watch?v=d9Yb6pQagHs

Pink Shirt Teammates
FEBRUARY 21

In 2007, Travis Price and DJ Shephard, seniors at Central Kings Rural High School at the time, made a good teammate move of epic proportions. What they did that day forever altered the course of history—*for the better.*

Price and Shepherd learned that Chuck McNeill, a ninth grader at their school, was being bullied for wearing a pink polo shirt on the first day of school. Bullies were harassing McNeil with homophobic insults and threatening to beat him up. So Price and Shepherd, who had themselves been bullied when they were younger, decided to take a stand.

The duo went out and bought dozens of pink shirts to hand out to Central King students. They then took to social media to encourage everyone at the school to wear pink the next day in support of the bullied McNeil.

When McNeil arrived for the second day of school, he was greeted by what Price and Shepherd described as a "sea of pink."

In an interview with the Canadian Museum for Human Rights, Price said: "You could see the weight that was lifted off (McNeil's) shoulders to know that he wasn't going to continue to be the bullied kid in school, that he was going to be just another kid in school, another student. He was going to be able to live his life."

The actions Price and Shepherd took that day back in 2007 would give birth to what is now known as Pink Shirt Day. Today, people from countries around the world wear pink shirts on the last Wednesday in February to signify a stand against bullying.

Pink Shirt Day falls during Anti-Bullying Week and occurs just days before International Stand Up to Bullying Day, which happens on the last Friday in February.

I wrote about the connection between good teammates and bullying in chapter 34. (Good teammates don't bully, nor do they tend to be bullied.)

If you've read *The WE Gear* or have ever heard me speak, you know I explain the art of being a good teammate through the acronym A.L.I.V.E. (Good teammates are Active, Loyal, Invested, Viral, and Empathetic.) Price and Shepherd illustrate the power of ALIVE teammates.

- They saw a problem and were **active** in solving it. They didn't blame, shame, or complain. They acted.

- They saw their school as their team and they were **loyal** to a teammate in need. Their allegiance was to something greater than themselves.

- They saw McNeil's problem as their problem and became **invested** in his problem.

- They saw an opportunity to share their passion and for it to spread to others. Wearing pink shirts and encouraging their fellow students to do the same made them **viral**.

- They saw that McNeil was hurting and made an effort to understand what it must feel like to be in his position. Their **empathy** led to a solution.

By being ALIVE, they turned bystanders into upstanders.

What I like best about the story of Pink Shirt Day is that neither Price nor Shepherd were popular kids at their school. They weren't part of the "in-crowd." They had no established platform nor position of influence. They were just two individuals inspired to bring about change.

Bullying is a problem that transcends schools. I have yet to encounter an underperforming team, be it sports, corporate, or other, that isn't plagued by some form of toxicity related to bullying. Many times, it is the members' responses—or lack of responses—to bullying that enable their teams' toxicity.

This week, follow Price and Shepherd's example. Take a courageous stand and don't let bullying hold you or your team back.

As always…Good teammates care. Good teammates share. Good teammates listen. Go be a good teammate.

A Motivated "Us"
FEBRUARY 28

A little over a month ago, I had the pleasure of speaking at a fundraising event for Southern Cross Service Dogs, an organization that provides trained service dogs at no cost to veterans with disabilities.

The "Always Beside You Gala" was an inspiring event born from an unfortunate premise.

Twenty-two veterans commit suicide every day. The compounded effects of post-traumatic stress, battle-related injuries, emotional trauma, and the sudden loss of a military identity leave many veterans experiencing a void in purpose.

Studies have shown that pairing these emotionally at-risk individuals with service dogs can enrich the quality of their lives and provide them with independence, fulfillment, and an increased sense of value.

Sadly, there is a shortage in the availability of trained service dogs. Not every veteran who could benefit from being paired with a service dog is able to get one. This is a problem—a *big* problem.

And like all big problems, this problem is best attacked through a team effort.

Southern Cross Service Dogs recognized that fact and is working to build a team that strives to provide service dogs that exemplify the motto "Always Beside You"—a motto I consider to, incidentally, be the perfect description of a good teammate.

At the gala, Josh Aronson, the Academy Award nominated director of the film *To Be of Service*, spoke about the incredible bond he witnessed between veterans suffering from post-traumatic stress and their service dogs.

Jon Bon Jovi thanked the audience for their support for the gala's worthy cause, before introducing the video for his song "Unbroken," which he wrote for the Aronson's film.

Cole Hauser, who plays Rip on the hit television show *Yellowstone*, auctioned off a trip to go horseback riding with him on the show's Montana set. (*FYI, former New York Yankee outfielder Johnny Damon made the winning bid!)

Everyone who attended the gala was interested in the event's mission. It was important, however, for them to be moved from being interested to invested.

Training service dogs is an expensive process. It can cost upwards of $50,000 to train a single dog. Without the financial means, there can be no mission.

When I took the stage at the gala, my charge was twofold:
1. Get the audience to see themselves as being part of the

Southern Cross team effort, and 2. Motivate the audience to become invested teammates.

I began by outlining the art of being a good teammate. I encouraged them to all become A.L.I.V.E. (Active, Loyal, Invested, Viral, and Empathetic) teammates and then ended my talk with the following assertion:

"When you get a group of *MEs* to become a *WE*, you create the most powerful catalyst for change on the planet—a *motivated US*. The veteran needs the dog. The dog needs Southern Cross. And Southern Cross needs *US*."

Whether it's an audience at a fundraising event, a sports team, a sales team, or a church congregation, creating a *motivated US* is always the best path to bringing about change. A *motivated US* takes ownership of the problem and pursues the solution with relentless resolve.

Service dogs bestow unconditional love, offer steadfast support, and provide unwavering companionship—just like a *motivated US*.

As always…Good teammates care. Good teammates share. Good teammates listen. Go be a good teammate.

Nice Job, Buddy
MARCH 7

Leaders often complain about jealousy upending their teams' chemistry. Someone on the team has achieved something that another team member covets. The feelings brought on by this scenario prevent the team from attaining a level of connectedness conducive to team success.

Surprisingly, I have seen *mimicry* upend just as many teams as jealousy.

Mimicry is when someone on the team copies something that another team member is doing. It could be a fashion style, strategy, or technique that has given the person being copied a unique identity and individual success.

Mimicry can cause the person being copied to feel angry, frustrated, and resentful—the same disruptive feelings brought on by jealousy.

Whenever I hear of someone struggling with mimicry, I am reminded of an experience I had in middle school.

My fifth-grade teacher, Mr. Mueller, was wonderfully creative. He utilized *outside-the-box* activities to teach his students useful life skills. Among my favorites was a public speaking project where he divided the class into small groups to be radio broadcast teams.

One student in each group was assigned to read the news headlines. Others were assigned jobs like giving the local weather, producing a commercial, and announcing the release of a new song. In my group, I was tasked with doing the sports report.

Mr. Mueller had us do a practice "broadcast" the day before we presented our final assignment. My group was the last to go that day. When I read the sports report, I did so by imitating Howard Cosell—a popular sportscaster at the time.

After I finished, the classroom was silent. Nobody else had done anything like that during their broadcast. They had all just used their regular voices.

I looked at Mr. Mueller, fearful that I had done something wrong. But Mr. Mueller was smiling. He jotted down a few notes and then turned to me and said, "Nice job, buddy."

The next day, everybody in the class used some form of an alternative voice when they presented their final projects with every sports report done in a Howard Cosell-esque voice. The imitations had become tiresome by the time it was my group's turn to present, especially for our teacher.

I felt conflicted. Should I do the Howard Cosell voice again now that everyone had done it? I suspect Mr. Mueller sensed my apprehension. His face conveyed an expression of curiosity, as if to say "Well, how are you going to handle this?"

I paused, thought about what to do, and then proceeded in my normal voice: "Often imitated, but never duplicated, this is the sports report with the one and only Lance Loya..."

When I finished, I looked at Mr. Mueller, who was smiling. He again jotted down a few notes before turning to me and saying, "Nice job, buddy."

I have never forgotten the lesson I learned that day in Mr. Mueller's class: Mimicry is good.

Imitation truly is the sincerest form of flattery. Not only that but being copied keeps you from plateauing. Mimicry compels innovation by forcing you out of your comfort zone.

If you're being copied by someone on your team, view it as a blessing instead of a burden. Adopting this mindset will lead to continued growth for you and your team—far more productive outcomes than anger, frustration, and resentment.

By the way...

Teachers who utilize creativity in their teaching repertoire are amazing. I spent a lot of time sharing the good teammate message at elementary schools last week for Read Across America events.

I was moved by the creativity I saw on display at those schools. It made me realize how fortunate I was to have had a teacher like Mr. Mueller.

If you're an educational leader, parent, or student who has encountered a "Mr. Mueller" in your life, be sure to tell them "Nice job, buddy."

And Mr. Mueller, wherever you are, thank you for teaching me such an invaluable lesson.

As always…Good teammates care. Good teammates share. Good teammates listen. Go be a good teammate.

Shoelace Empowerment
MARCH 14

I got to have lunch recently with my friend Sister Eric Marie, the octogenarian nun that I wrote about in my book *Building Good Teammates: The Story of My Mount Rushmore, a Coaching Epiphany, and That Nun.*

We were joined by two of Sister Eric Marie's friends, Sister Benedict and Sister Giuseppe.

Realizing that I was surrounded by generational wisdom, I asked them what they considered to be some of their lives' greatest victories. Sister Giuseppe provided an inspiring and insightful response.

Sister Giuseppe spent her professional career working with preschoolers. She's had a front row seat to some of the most comical moments known to mankind. In many, many ways, her life has been a living, breathing episode of *Kids Say the Darndest Things.*

But amid those comical interactions, nestled between teaching kids their ABCs, shapes, and colors were triumphant moments that mold the human heart.

To explain her greatest victory, Sister Giuseppe told a story about how she taught a boy with one hand to tie his shoes.

Most of us learn to tie our shoes though some method involving bunny ears or a clever rhyme about swooping, looping, and going down a hole. Those conventional strategies, however, require the use of two hands. Teaching a child to tie their shoes with one hand necessitates a different approach.

As Sister Giuseppe laid the framework for her story, I found myself wondering how I would tackle her problem—the way I suspect you are right now. We would probably begin by searching Google and then maybe watching a few YouTube "how to" videos before attempting to apply what we had learned.

But in the Pre-Internet era, Sister Giuseppe didn't have those tools at her disposal. She had to rely on her own ingenuity. Sister Giuseppe devoted countless extra hours working with her one-handed boy until he finally got it.

When Sister Giuseppe finished her story, I realized that *how* she solved the problem didn't matter to me nearly as much as *why* she viewed solving it among her life's biggest victories.

Learning to tie one's own shoes is a childhood rite of passage. Not being able to reach that benchmark with his peers would have been crushing to that boy's attitude toward his physical state.

Sister Giuseppe couldn't allow herself to let that happen, so she chose to see the boy's problem as her problem. That choice took her outside of her comfort zone, tested the limits of her patience, and brought her added aggravation. Yet it made a tremendous difference at a pivotal time in that boy's life.

By becoming an invested teammate, she empowered the boy with the knowledge that he could overcome his physical shortcomings and that they did not have to be a source of confinement. Her investment set him up for a life of optimism.

Sister Giuseppe's story demonstrates the value gained from having a mentor invest in you. The fact that she considers that moment to be her greatest victory, decades removed from it happening, also demonstrates the value a mentor gains from investing in others.

In the end, it won't be the wealth you amass nor the possessions you acquire that matter to you the most. It will be the impact you had on the lives of those you encountered.

As always…Good teammates care. Good teammates share. Good teammates listen. Go be a good teammate.

Four Ways to Crush Cliques
MARCH 21

Cliques—tightknit groups within the primary team that engage in exclusivity by ostracizing those outside of their group—destroy teams from the inside out. They undermine culture, hurt morale, and cripple productivity.

But more than anything, cliques keep teams from performing at their optimum level.

Here are four ways to crush cliques:

1. **Provide an Outlet to Vent.** Frustration is one of the primary reasons why cliques form. People are frustrated with something that is happening on their team and they have a growing need to convey those frustrations. When they don't have an avenue to do so, it can cause their frustrations to fester and trigger them to seek the solace of other malcontents.

   By providing team members with an outlet to vent, you release the pressure brought on by their frustrations and eliminate the need for them to commiserate through unhealthy means. Care committees, suggestion boxes, discussions groups, or empathic ears can all serve this purpose.

2. **Taboo Gossip.** Assuming everyone on the team knows that gossip is detrimental to the team is a mistake. Assuming that everyone on the team knows the difference between gossip and venting is also a mistake.

   Healthy venting creates awareness, releases stress, and can lead to solutions. Gossip—talking about a person who isn't present—promotes toxicity, reduces inclusivity, and can lead to rumors.

   Be proactive about letting others know that gossip is taboo on your team. Mention it during team meetings. Post signs reminding team members about it. Include it in your teams' social media profiles and email signatures. Everyone on the team should realize that they are breaking a sacred team rule if they choose to gossip.

3. **Steer the Socialization.** According to a study published in *Social Psychological and Personality Science*, the typical person spends about fifty-two minutes per day gossiping. That same study revealed that not everything that was "gossiped" about was malicious.

   Humans have an innate need to socialize, which makes gossip an instinctive practice. What is talked about around the water cooler doesn't necessarily matter as much as the actual act of conversing. A CareerBuilder survey showed that twenty percent of workers said they've done something they didn't want to do, like gossiping, just to fit in with co-workers.

Team leaders can steer the socialization by offering a daily topic of discussion (*Which fast food restaurant has the best French fries? What song had the biggest impact on the world? Who made the best Batman?*) There's only so much time available for gossip. You reduce the opportunity for poisonous discussions if you can monopolize that time with alternative topics.

4. **Cross-Pollinate.** Not all cliques are born from dissatisfaction. Sometimes people flock to familiarity (i.e., class, position, department, etc.)

   In my book *The WE Gear*, I recount a story about an issue the Foster Grandparent Program was having with cliques. The source of their cliquey behavior was not malcontent, it was comfort. These kindhearted seniors only wanted to work with those they already knew and felt comfortable around.

   By cross-pollinating, intermixing individuals from different factions, you expand familiarity and create new comfort zones. You also strengthen team bonds.

   I know of a leader who deliberately walks into team meetings late, just so she can rotate team members to different seats. Her practice exposes her staff to new ways of thinking, broadens connections, and diminishes cliques.

Whether you provide an outlet to vent, taboo gossip, steer socialization or cross-pollinate, know that your efforts to keep cliques from contaminating your team will always be a good teammate move on your part and edge your team closer to reaching its full potential.

As always…Good teammates care. Good teammates share. Good teammates listen. Go be a good teammate.

The Social Psychological and Science study referenced above is from Robbins, M. L., and Karan, A. (2020). "Who Gossips and How in Everyday Life?" Social Psychological and Personality Science, 11(2). https://doi.org/10.1177/1948550619837000

**The CareerBuilder survey referenced above can be found at https://press.careerbuilder.com/2013-07-24-Forty-three-Percent-of-Workers-Say-their-Office-has-Cliques-Finds-CareerBuilder-Survey*

Marliese the Photographer
MARCH 28

Marliese Marie is a brilliant photographer. She works closely with acting and modeling agencies in commercial hotbeds like New York, Atlanta, Miami, Orlando, and Los Angeles.

Clients find her to be creative, personable, and exceptionally gifted at capturing the "right" moment. In her hands, a camera is wielded like a wizard's wand.

I had the chance recently to watch Marliese employ her magic during a photoshoot for an upcoming project and I became instantly enamored with her process.

Most photographers are quick to assert their vision for the shoot onto the subject. But Marliese seemed more interested in learning about my vision. She wanted to know how I wanted to be seen in the photos.

"Is there a word to describe the look you're after?" she asked.

I thought about her question and said, "Approachable." I help team leaders create better individual teammates. They will be reluctant to bring their issues to me if I don't seem approachable.

Marliese nodded her head, asked a few follow up questions, pondered each of my responses, and then went to work. What ensued was an enlightening exercise in trust, empathy, and the art of being a good teammate.

I knew I couldn't control the sightlines Marliese chose, how close she zoomed, nor the way she manipulated the backgrounds. I had to rely on her expertise—which required trust.

She knew she couldn't just assert her creativity onto the project. She had to first gain an understanding of my objectives—which required empathy.

The combination of my trust and her empathy enabled our rapport—which transformed my vision and her vision into *our* vision.

Marliese's willingness to see challenges through another's lens, if you'll pardon the pun, is precisely what makes her a good photographer. It is also what makes her a good teammate.

You will fail as a teammate if you only see others' challenges from your perspective. To be an effective member of your team, you must endeavor to see your teammates' challenges from *their* perspective.

You'll also fail as a teammate if you don't trust the other members of your team. To be an effective team member, you must endeavor to have faith in your teammates.

As always…Good teammates care. Good teammates share. Good teammates listen. Go be a good teammate.

A.N.T. Monitors
APRIL 4

Good teammates monitor their ANT populations.

Renowned physician and psychiatrist Dr. Daniel Amen coined the term ANT (Automatic Negative Thought) in the early 1990s. After an especially tough day of dealing with suicidal patients, troubled teens, and contentious married couples, the *New York Times* bestselling author of *Change Your Brain, Change Your Life* came home to discover that his kitchen had been overrun by an ant infestation.

None of the insects were an imposing problem on their own, but en masse they were a formidable foe.

While battling the infestation with wet paper towels, it occurred to Dr. Amen that the patients he had seen earlier that day were embroiled in a comparable situation. Their anxiety, depression, and grief were the result of their minds being overrun by negative thoughts. (e.g., *This will never work out. Things will never be the same. I'll never get used to this new normal. I'm a loser, etc.*)

Although the negative thoughts were in many ways a natural reaction to the circumstances, their abundance was causing a biochemical change in his patients' brains. The ANTs were robbing his patients of joy and propelling them into a downward mental spiral.

On the Positive University Podcast, Dr. Amen discussed how certain conditions can cause ANT populations to surge.

"ANT populations go up when you haven't slept. ANT populations go up in women the week before they start their period. ANT populations go up when you're withdrawing from alcohol or marijuana. ANT populations go up when you haven't eaten in a while," Amen said.

From a good teammate perspective, how you monitor conditions that are conducive to an increase in ANT populations can define how good of a teammate you are.

Take the issue of not eating in a while. Not eating drops blood sugar, which reduces blood flow to the frontal lobe— the area of the brain responsible for higher cognitive functions like memory, impulse control, problem solving, and social interaction.

This condition alters the body's biochemical composition and invites ANTs to enter your mind. It is the equivalent of leaving an open pack of sugar on a kitchen counter.

Hangry people aren't good teammates because they're overrun with negative thoughts. Their downward spiral makes them increasingly irritable, irrational, and emotionally volatile.

Good teammates are aware of this reality, so they take precautions to keep themselves and their fellow teammates from entering a state of *hangriness*. They plan meals in advance, stick to a mealtime schedule, and carry snacks in case that schedule is unexpectedly disrupted.

Anyone who has ever had to deal with a hangry teammate knows how impactful of a good teammate move it can be to have some snack crackers on hand.

Good teammates employ similar strategies for issues related to lack of sleep, substance withdrawal, or any other detrimental conditions. They understand that prevention is always a better strategy than reaction—especially when it comes to ANT populations.

As always…Good teammates care. Good teammates share. Good teammates listen. Go be a good teammate.

*The full Positive University podcast episode referenced above can be found at https://positiveuniversity.com/episode/dr-amen/

A Recipe for Disappointment
APRIL 11

Have you ever tried to replicate a menu item from a popular restaurant? Maybe Outback Steakhouse's Bloomin' Onion? Cinnabon's Cinnamon Buns? Texas Roadhouse's Hot Rolls? Starbucks' Pink Drink?

Discovering one of these coveted secret recipes holds a certain allure. Why be inconvenienced by having to leave your house when you can create the same deliciousness in your own kitchen? And why pay more for something that you can create on your own for a fraction of what it costs at the restaurant?

If so called "copycat recipes" work out for you the way they do for me, you know the answers to those questions: Because the version you make at home never quite tastes the same as the real thing. You are always left disappointed.

The problem with most copycat recipes is that they give you the *how*, but not the *what*—the minutia that molds the finished product.

Let's say you discover a recipe for your favorite restaurant's famous apple dumplings. The recipe calls for flour, butter, sugar, cinnamon, and apples. It includes the appropriate measurements, oven temperature, and baking time.

You follow all the steps, yet your dumplings don't taste as good as the ones served at your favorite restaurant. They're "a little off" because the recipe was missing a few crucial details.

For instance, what brand of flour, butter, sugar, and cinnamon does the restaurant use? What type of pan do they use? What type of apples do they use? Using the right apples makes a difference. Golden delicious apples taste different than Granny Smith or Gala.

The seemingly insignificant details of the *what* matter. Team leaders can sometimes find themselves facing a situation akin to this when trying to improve teamwork and create good teammates. They become so focused on the expedience of the *how* that they overlook the importance of the *what*.

The recipe for creating good teammates is rather simple:

1. Provide your team with a definition of a good teammate.
2. Emphasize the desired behaviors.
3. Recognize when those behaviors are displayed.
4. Reward team members who display them.
5. Repeat.

But if you don't the use right definition (the *what*) or aren't emphasizing, recognizing, or rewarding behaviors the right way (the *what*), your results will also end up being "a little off."

Much of the work I do involves getting team leaders to understand that terms like *the we gear, clutch moments,* and *good teammate moves* matter. They're the important minutiae and implementing them can be the difference between having a winning culture and fledgling one.

The best team leaders strive to be good teammates to those they lead. They realize that providing their team the *how* without also providing them the *what* is a recipe for disappointment. That's why they make the extra effort to seek the details that others overlook.

As always…Good teammates care. Good teammates share. Good teammates listen. Go be a good teammate.

Responding to Distress Calls
APRIL 18

On April 18, 1912, Captain Arthur Roston guided the RMS Carpathia into the New York City Harbor. Aboard his ship were the 705 passengers he and his crew had rescued from the sunken RMS Titanic three days prior.

The Titanic was heralded as the "unsinkable" ship. That it had succumbed to tragedy on its maiden voyage was simply unfathomable.

Roston had already retired to his cabin when the Carpathia's wireless operator woke him with news of the Titanic's distress call. Upon learning about the Titanic's predicament, the captain immediately rerouted his ship to assist the sinking ocean liner.

The Carpathia's prompt and heroic response that fateful night are indicative of how good teammates accept two inherent elements that accompany responding to a distress call: sacrifice and risk.

Sacrifice

Assisting a teammate in distress requires sacrifice on your part. Surrendering comfort and convenience can be expected.

The Carpathia was 58 miles away from the Titanic when it received the distress call. Roston ordered the heating, hot water, and electricity to all cabins and common areas shut off to increase his ship's top speed.

This measure left Carpathia's passengers to contend with the North Atlantic's frigid temperatures and a rougher ride, but it allowed the steam vessel to increase its maximum speed from 14 knots to what was at the time an amazing 18 knots—expediting the Carpathia's arrival by an hour.

Additionally, Carpathia's passengers and crew sacrificed sleep to ready the ship for the survivors. They gave up their staterooms, shared clothes and blankets, and helped convert the ship's dining halls into makeshift hospitals.

Risk

Assisting a teammate in distress involves the assumption of risk. You could get hurt physically, emotionally, and/or socially.

The Carpathia reported passing six large icebergs on its way to the Titanic. Traveling at an accelerated speed, without radar, in the dark, in treacherous waters could have also resulted in tragedy for Roston's ship.

By insisting on bringing aboard every Titanic survivor they could find, the considerably smaller Carpathia doubled its passenger count. Space limitations forced the Carpathia to abandon seven lifeboats at the wreckage site, which left the ship with too few lifeboats to accommodate all its passengers in the event of an emergency—the exact problem the Titanic encountered.

No one ever knows the extent of the good that can come from responding to a distress call.

Twenty-eight years after the Carpathia responded to the Titanic's call, the German army had trapped nearly 400,000 British troops in the French port city of Dunkirk. The port's shallow waters prevented larger British destroyers from approaching the Dunkirk beaches.

Aware that his troops would be annihilated if not quickly evacuated, British Prime Minister Winston Churchill issued a distress call of his own, asking for privately-owned small boats and yachts to help ferry Dunkirk soldiers back across the English Channel.

Charles Lightoller, a 66-year-old retiree, was among the civilian boat owners who responded to Churchill's plea. Lightoller's response inspired others to respond. He's considered by many historians to be among the operation's biggest heroes.

Mark Rylance's character in the film *Dunkirk* was based on Lightoller—who happened to be the final Titanic survivor pulled aboard the Carpathia.

The next time you receive a distress call, think about the connection between the Titanic and the event that Churchill would come to refer to as the "Miracle of Dunkirk." How you respond today could influence the miracles of tomorrow.

As always…Good teammates care. Good teammates share. Good teammates listen. Go be a good teammate.

Bring the Good Teammate
Message to Your Team

Are you interested in bringing the "Good Teammate" message to your event or implementing strategies to improve the quality of the teammates you have on your team? If so, contact Lance Loya at:

Phone: (814) 659-9605

E-mail: info@coachloya.com

Website: www.coachloya.com

Twitter: @coachlanceloya

Facebook: facebook.com/coachloya

Instagram: @coachlanceloya

LinkedIn: linkedin.com/in/coachloya

Join the movement and sign up for Lance Loya's weekly *Teammate Tuesday* blog at *www.coachloya.com/blog.*

*If you have enjoyed this book or it has inspired you in some way, we would love to hear from you! Be a good teammate and *share* your photos and stories with us through email or social media. We want to hear from you!

About the Author

Lance Loya is the founder and CEO of The Good Teammate Factory and the creator of National Be a Good Teammate Day. As a leading authority on team dynamics, he specializes in getting individuals to shift their focus from *me* to *we*. Other experts concentrate on improving teamwork, but Lance concentrates on improving the teammate. Lance's method works!

Lance has authored ten books on the subject of being a good teammate. His book *The WE Gear* topped *Forbes'* list of "20 Books to Make You a Better Coach or Mentor."

A college basketball coach turned best-selling author, blogger, podcaster, and professional speaker, he is known for his enthusiastic personality and his passion for turning *teambusters* into good teammates.

When not speaking or writing, he is a loyal husband to his high school sweetheart and a doting father to his two daughters—who, incidentally, were the impetus behind his heartwarming children's book.

Also by Lance Loya

Be a Good Teammate

Building Good Teammates

Teammate Tuesdays

Teammate Tuesdays Volume II

The WE Gear

Teammate Tuesdays Volume III

Outside the Box, Within the Cube

Teammate Tuesdays Volume IV

Teammate Tuesdays Volume V

Celebrate Your Teammates

Good teammates make being part of the team worthwhile! That's why on July 22, **National Be a Good Teammate Day** recognizes the sacrifices, kindness, and generosity of these selfless individuals.

Whether it's sports, family, community, school, or work, everybody is part of a team. Use the day to show your appreciation to those willing to put the needs of their "team" ahead of themselves.

Honor their contributions to the team with a boisterous "Thank you!" or a well-deserved high five or hug. Be sure to let the world know how grateful you are by sharing a photo of you and a good teammate on social media, using the hashtag:

#NationalBeAGoodTeammateDay

Listen to the Podcast

Do you like to listen to podcasts during your daily commute or while you work out? Check out The Good Teammate Podcast! Listening to Lance Loya discuss the art of being a good teammate through short audio selections from his *Teammate Tuesday* blog is guaranteed to inject a dose of happiness into your life.

The Be a Good Teammate Podcast is available on Apple Podcasts, Google Podcasts, Amazon Music, Spotify, TuneIn Radio, and Anchor.

You can download past episodes or subscribe to receive notifications about the release of new episodes. To learn more, visit:

www.coachloya.com/podcast/

Learn from a Course

THE GOOD TEAMMATE FACTORY

The Good Teammate Factory offers online video courses to help teams gain greater insight in the art of being a good teammate. Courses are available for both sports and corporate teams and are an ideal way to improve teamwork, reduce selfishness, and draw teams closer together.

Teams engage in the course content and activities together in a group setting such as a meeting room or classroom. The courses are flexible in that they can be completed in a single sitting or divided up and stretched out over a series of meetings.

If you want to improve teamwork, send your team to The Good Teammate Factory!

WWW.GOODTEAMMATEFACTORY.COM

Are *you* a good teammate? Your team's potential for achieving success is ultimately dependent upon your answer to this question. Everybody wants teamwork on their team, but teamwork doesn't happen without good teammates—individuals who prioritize team objectives over personal agendas.

Gaining insight into the kind of a teammate you are increases your awareness for how your actions impact the other members of your team. It also increases the likelihood of your team working together to achieve genuine synergy.

Take the good teammate quiz today to assess your aptitude for practicing good teammate behaviors! To learn more about the quiz, visit:

www.coachloya.com/quiz/

Made in the USA
Middletown, DE
04 February 2025